Full-Stack Development with Python & React

Build Dynamic Web Apps with Django, FastAPI, and Modern Front-End Frameworks

Thompson Carter

Rafael Sanders

Miguel Farmer

Contents

Chapter 8: Handling Real-Time Data with WebSockets and React.............................. 180

[13]

Chapter 12: Deploying Full-Stack Web Applications 274

How to Scan a Barcode to Get a Repository

1. **Install a QR/Barcode Scanner** – Ensure you have a barcode or QR code scanner app installed on your smartphone or use a built-in scanner in **GitHub, GitLab, or Bitbucket.**

2. **Open the Scanner** – Launch the scanner app and grant necessary camera permissions.

3. **Scan the Barcode** – Align the barcode within the scanning frame. The scanner will automatically detect and process it.

4. **Follow the Link** – The scanned result will display a **URL to the repository**. Tap the link to open it in your web browser or Git client.

5. **Clone the Repository** – Use **Git clone** with the provided URL to download the repository to your local machine.

[16]

Chapter 1: Introduction to Full-Stack Development

1.1 Understanding Full-Stack Development

What is Full-Stack Development?

At its core, full-stack development refers to the process of building both the front-end and back-end of web applications. In simpler terms, it's like constructing an entire building—front-end developers design and create the visible part (the user-facing side), while back-end developers focus on the inner workings, making sure everything runs smoothly behind the scenes.

The front-end is everything that users interact with directly, such as web pages, buttons, and forms. It's where the user experience happens. The back-end, on the other hand, handles the logic, database management, and server-side interactions. Full-stack development encompasses both sides, meaning that a full-stack developer is someone who can work on both the front-end and back-end of an application.

The term "full-stack" refers to the entire technology stack that a developer uses to build these applications. This stack can include programming languages, frameworks, databases, and tools required to develop both the front-end and back-end.

Key Responsibilities of a Full-Stack Developer

A full-stack developer wears many hats. They must be skilled in both front-end and back-end technologies and are responsible for:

1. **Building and Maintaining Front-End Components**: This includes creating user interfaces, implementing designs, and making sure the user experience is seamless.

2. **Developing Back-End Logic**: Full-stack developers write the logic that handles the requests, processes data, and manages interactions with the database. They also handle the application's authentication, data storage, and server-side functionalities.

3. **Working with Databases**: Full-stack developers set up, maintain, and interact with databases that store the data used by the application. They design schemas, manage queries, and ensure that data is efficiently retrieved and stored.

4. **Connecting Front-End and Back-End**: Full-stack developers integrate the front-end with the back-end, ensuring that data is passed smoothly between the two. They build APIs and work with protocols to make sure everything works together.

5. **Deployment and Maintenance**: Once the application is developed, full-stack developers also handle deployment, ensuring that the application runs on a server and is maintained over time.

6. **Ensuring Security and Scalability**: Full-stack developers ensure that the

application is secure from potential vulnerabilities and can scale to accommodate growing user bases or data loads.

To put it simply, full-stack developers are like a team of specialists rolled into one. They work on all the layers of an application, from the user interface to the database, and ensure that everything runs smoothly from start to finish.

The Importance of Full-Stack Development in the Modern Web

The modern web is incredibly dynamic, with businesses and individuals demanding more sophisticated web applications. Full-stack development is essential because it provides a complete, holistic approach to web development. Here's why full-stack developers are in high demand:

1. **Versatility**: Full-stack developers can work on both the front-end and back-end, making them highly adaptable. They are capable of handling all aspects of a project, which reduces the need for separate teams or developers for different layers of the application.

2. **Efficiency and Speed**: A full-stack developer's ability to handle both sides of development makes the process quicker and more efficient. It also simplifies communication between the front-end and back-end, leading to faster development cycles.

3. **Cost-Effectiveness**: By hiring a single full-stack developer instead of multiple specialized developers, businesses can reduce overhead costs.

4. **End-to-End Control**: Full-stack developers have control over the entire process, from design to deployment. This allows for greater consistency in the application and a more seamless user experience.

5. **Cross-Disciplinary Knowledge**: Full-stack developers understand both the user-facing side and the behind-the-scenes logic, which leads to better decision-making regarding performance, security, and usability.

In a world where speed, adaptability, and cost-efficiency matter, full-stack development is critical for building modern, dynamic, and scalable web applications.

1.2 The Components of Full-Stack Development

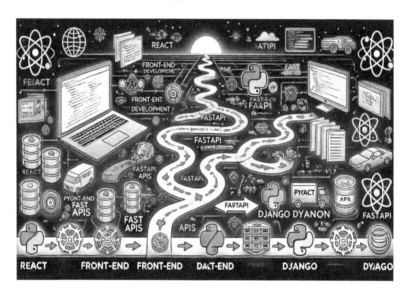

Front-End Technologies: React

The front-end is everything the user interacts with. Front-end technologies are essential for creating user interfaces that are visually appealing and interactive. One of the most popular tools for building modern, dynamic web interfaces is **React**.

React is a JavaScript library developed by Facebook for building user interfaces, particularly single-page applications (SPAs) where the page reloads dynamically without refreshing the entire page. React enables developers to build complex, interactive UIs using simple, reusable components.

Here's an overview of React's key concepts:

1. **Components**: React is built around the concept of components—self-contained pieces of code that manage their state and render themselves based on that state. Components can be reused and composed together to build entire applications.

2. **JSX**: JSX is a syntax extension for JavaScript that looks like HTML but allows you to embed JavaScript logic within HTML-like code. It's the foundation of

React components and makes it easy to write and understand React code.

3. **State and Props**: In React, **state** is used to store data that can change over time, like user inputs. **Props** are how data is passed between components.

4. **React Hooks**: Hooks are functions that let you "hook into" React features like state and lifecycle methods without writing a class-based component.

Example: A Simple React Component

```jsx
jsx

import React, { useState } from 'react';

function Counter() {
  const [count, setCount] =
useState(0);
```

```
  return (
    <div>
      <p>Count: {count}</p>
      <button onClick={() =>
setCount(count +
1)}>Increment</button>
    </div>
  );
}

export default Counter;
```

In this simple React component, the button increments the counter each time it's clicked, and the count updates on the page.

React allows for faster development and is highly scalable for complex applications, making it a popular choice for modern front-end development.

Back-End Technologies: Django and FastAPI

The back-end is where the logic and data processing happen. It is responsible for handling requests from the front-end, processing them, and sending back the appropriate responses. Two of the most popular frameworks for building back-end applications in Python are **Django** and **FastAPI**.

Django is a high-level Python web framework that encourages rapid development and clean, pragmatic design. It comes with many built-in features, including an ORM (Object-Relational Mapping) system for interacting with databases, user authentication, and admin interfaces.

FastAPI, on the other hand, is a modern, high-performance web framework for building APIs with Python. It's especially known for its speed and its use of Python type hints, which makes it a great choice for building **REST**ful **API**s quickly.

Here's a brief comparison of the two:

1. **Django**:
   - Built-in admin interface.
   - Works well for full-fledged applications.
   - Comes with a lot of "batteries included," including tools for authentication, database management, and more.

2. **FastAPI**:
   - Designed for building fast APIs.
   - Handles asynchronous programming and concurrency natively.

○ Supports automatic API documentation via Swagger UI.

Both frameworks are excellent choices, and the choice between them depends on the needs of the application. If you're building a complex web app with many features, Django may be the way to go. If you need a fast, asynchronous API, FastAPI is an excellent choice.

Databases and Cloud Infrastructure

A critical aspect of full-stack development is managing data. **Databases** are essential for storing and retrieving data for web applications, while **cloud infrastructure** allows you to deploy and scale your applications.

1. **Databases**: Full-stack developers work with both relational databases (like **PostgreSQL** or **MySQL**) and non-relational databases (like **MongoDB**). Relational databases are

ideal for structured data and support **SQL** queries, while **NoSQL** databases are better for unstructured or semi-structured data.

2. **Cloud Infrastructure**: Cloud providers like **AWS**, **Google Cloud**, and **Azure** allow full-stack developers to deploy their applications in a scalable, cost-effective way. Cloud services handle everything from server management to storage and databases, so developers can focus on building applications.

Connecting Front-End and Back-End: The Full-Stack Workflow

Now that we understand the technologies involved in full-stack development, let's discuss how the front-end and back-end work together. A key component of full-stack development is **APIs**

(Application Programming Interfaces), which allow the front-end and back-end to communicate.

For example, when a user submits a form in a React application, the front-end sends an HTTP request to the back-end (Django or FastAPI). The back-end processes the request (such as saving the data to a database) and sends a response back to the front-end, which updates the UI accordingly.

This process is what makes dynamic web applications function, and understanding how the front-end and back-end work together is crucial for any full-stack developer.

1.3 Real-World Use Cases for Full-Stack Development

Healthcare Apps

In healthcare, full-stack developers are responsible for building applications that store and process sensitive patient data, manage appointments, and enable communication between doctors and patients. A common example is a telemedicine platform, where a doctor and patient can connect via video calls, and the system manages patient records and appointment scheduling.

E-Commerce Platforms

E-commerce platforms like **Amazon** or **Etsy** rely heavily on full-stack development. Full-stack developers build the user interface, implement features like searching and filtering products, and handle back-end tasks like order processing, inventory management, and payment integration.

Logistics & Inventory Management

In logistics, full-stack developers work on systems that track shipments, manage inventory, and process orders in real-time. These applications may require complex data management and integration with external services like shipping providers or warehouse systems.

Social Media Platforms

Full-stack development is also critical for building social media platforms like **Facebook** or **Twitter**, where developers need to manage user data, handle posts, manage real-time communication, and integrate features like notifications and messaging.

Conclusion

In this chapter, we've explored the essentials of full-stack development: what it is, the key responsibilities of a full-stack developer, the components involved (like front-end and back-end technologies), and real-world use cases. Full-stack development allows you to build complete, functional web applications and is a vital skill in today's web development landscape.

In the following chapters, we'll dive deeper into the specific technologies that make up the full-stack, giving you the knowledge and hands-on experience needed to start building dynamic web apps from the ground up.

Chapter 2: Getting Started with Python for Web Development

2.1 Introduction to Python and Its Role in Web Development

Why Python for Web Development?

Python has become one of the most popular programming languages in the world. It's known for its simplicity, readability, and versatility, making it an excellent choice for beginners and professionals alike. But why has Python become so widely adopted in web development?

1. **Ease of Learning**: Python's syntax is simple and easy to understand. Its clean structure

allows developers to focus on solving problems rather than grappling with complex code.

2. **Wide Range of Libraries and Frameworks**: Python has an extensive collection of libraries and frameworks that make web development faster and easier. These include **Django** and **Flask** for building web applications and APIs, as well as tools for database management, user authentication, and much more.

3. **Versatility**: Python is used not only for web development but also for data science, machine learning, automation, and more. This makes it an incredibly valuable skill for developers looking to work in different fields.

4. **Strong Community Support**: With a large and active community, Python developers

have access to a wealth of tutorials, forums, and open-source projects. Whether you're a beginner or an experienced developer, you'll always find support when working with Python.

5. **Cross-Platform Compatibility**: Python is cross-platform, meaning you can write code that runs on Windows, macOS, and Linux without modification. This makes it an ideal choice for developers who need to create applications that run on multiple platforms.

Overview of Python Web Frameworks

When it comes to web development, Python has several powerful frameworks that simplify the process of building robust applications. Two of the most popular Python web frameworks are **Django** and **Flask**. Let's take a quick look at both:

1. **Django**:

   o **Full-Featured Framework**: Django is a high-level, full-stack web framework. It comes with a lot of built-in features, including an ORM (Object-Relational Mapping), authentication system, and an admin panel, all of which speed up the development process.

   o **Rapid Development**: With Django, you can quickly build complex, database-driven websites. It follows the "batteries-included" philosophy, meaning you get a lot of built-in functionality that you can customize to suit your needs.

- ○ **Security Features**: Django comes with built-in security features like protection against SQL injection, cross-site scripting (XSS), and cross-site request forgery (CSRF).

2. **Flask:**

- ○ **Micro-Framework**: Flask is a lightweight framework that is often referred to as a "micro-framework." It doesn't come with as many built-in tools as Django, but it offers more flexibility, allowing you to choose the tools and libraries you want to integrate.

- ○ **Minimalistic and Flexible**: Flask is ideal for smaller applications or when you want more control over the components of your app. It is also easier to get started with, making it a good choice for beginners.

○ **Extensions**: While Flask is minimal by design, it can be extended with various plugins to add features like authentication, database integration, and form handling.

Installing Python and Setting Up Your Development Environment

Before we dive into coding, let's get your development environment set up. Whether you're on Windows, macOS, or Linux, the steps for installing Python are straightforward.

1. **Installing Python**:

   ○ **Windows**: Go to the official Python website and download the latest version of Python for Windows. During installation, ensure you check the box to "Add Python to PATH."

   ○ **macOS**: Python comes pre-installed on macOS, but it's often an older version. You can install the latest version using the Homebrew package manager:

bash

```
brew install python
```

- o **Linux**: Most Linux distributions come with Python pre-installed. If not, you can install it using the following command:

```bash

sudo apt install python3
```

2. **Setting Up a Code Editor**: A good code editor makes a huge difference in your productivity. **VSCode** and **PyCharm** are two popular choices among Python developers.

  - o **VSCode**: Free, lightweight, and highly customizable. You can install Python extensions for linting, formatting, and debugging.

  - o **PyCharm**: A powerful IDE with more built-in features, including support for Django and Flask, as well as advanced debugging tools.

3. **Installing Required Libraries**: Once you've installed Python and a code editor, the next step is to install the necessary libraries for web development. For Django, you can install it via pip:

bash

```
pip install django
```

For Flask, use:

bash

```
pip install flask
```

2.2 Python Basics Refresher

Python Syntax and Data Structures

If you're new to Python or need a quick refresher, here's a rundown of Python syntax and data structures that are most commonly used in web development.

1. **Variables**: Variables are used to store data. In Python, you don't need to declare the data type of a variable. Python automatically infers the type based on the value you assign to it.

python

```
my_name = "John Doe"
age = 30
height = 5.9
```

2. **Data Types:**

   o **Strings**: Text data is stored in strings.

- o **Integers and Floats**: Numbers are either integers or floating-point numbers.

- o **Lists**: Lists are ordered collections of items, like arrays in other programming languages.

- o **Dictionaries**: Dictionaries store data in key-value pairs.

- o **Tuples**: Tuples are similar to lists but are immutable (unchangeable).

Example of a dictionary:

```python
person = {
    "name": "John Doe",
    "age": 30,
    "city": "New York"
}
```

3. **Conditionals**: Python uses if, elif, and else statements to execute code based on certain conditions.

```python
python
```

```python
if age >= 18:
    print("You are an adult.")
else:
    print("You are a minor.")
```

4. **Loops:**

   o **For Loop**: Used for iterating over sequences like lists or dictionaries.

   o **While Loop**: Repeats as long as a certain condition is true.

Example:

```python
python
```

```python
for item in person:
```

```python
    print(f"{item}:
{person[item]}")
```

5. **Functions**: Functions are reusable blocks of code. They allow you to perform tasks repeatedly without rewriting the same code.

Example:

python

```python
def greet(name):
    print(f"Hello, {name}!")

greet("Alice")
```

6. **Modules**: Modules are files containing Python definitions and statements. You can import and use them in your program.

python

```python
import math
```

```
print(math.sqrt(16))
```

Error Handling and Debugging

Error handling is an essential part of writing robust Python applications. You can handle errors gracefully using **try-except** blocks.

Example of error handling:

```python

try:
    result = 10 / 0
except ZeroDivisionError:
    print("Cannot divide by zero!")
```

Python also offers several debugging tools. The most common one is the **pdb** (Python Debugger), which allows you to set breakpoints and inspect the values of variables.

To use pdb:

```python

import pdb
pdb.set_trace()
```

2.3 Working with Virtual Environments

Why Use Virtual Environments?

Virtual environments allow you to create isolated environments for different projects, which helps prevent conflicts between package versions. This is especially useful when working on multiple projects that require different versions of libraries.

Without a virtual environment, installing a package globally can cause issues if one project needs a different version of the package than another.

Setting Up and Managing Virtual Environments with venv

Python provides a built-in tool called **venv** to create virtual environments. Here's how to set one up:

1. **Create a Virtual Environment**: In your project directory, run:

bash

```
python3 -m venv myenv
```

This creates a directory called myenv where Python and its dependencies will be installed.

2. **Activate the Virtual Environment:**

   ○ On **Windows**, run:

```bash
```

```
myenv\Scripts\activate
```

   ○ On **macOS** and **Linux**, run:

```bash
```

```
source myenv/bin/activate
```

3. Once activated, the name of your virtual environment will appear in the terminal prompt.

4. **Install Packages:** With the virtual environment activated, you can install libraries like Django or Flask:

```bash
```

```
pip install django
```

5. **Deactivate the Virtual Environment**: When you're done, you can deactivate the environment by simply running:

```bash
```

```
deactivate
```

Conclusion

In this chapter, we've introduced Python and its role in web development, covered the basics of Python syntax, and walked you through the process of setting up your development environment and using virtual environments. Understanding these foundational concepts is essential for any aspiring Python web developer.

Next, we'll dive into web development frameworks like Django and Flask, where you'll learn how to build your first Python web application.

Chapter 3: Back-End Development with Django

3.1 Introduction to Django

What is Django and Why Use It?

Django is a high-level web framework written in Python that simplifies the process of building complex, database-driven websites. It follows the "batteries-included" philosophy, meaning it comes with everything you need to get started with web development, right out of the box. Whether you're building a small application or a large-scale system, Django provides a solid foundation that allows developers to focus on writing unique code rather than reinventing the wheel.

Here are a few reasons why Django is one of the most popular frameworks for back-end web development:

1. **Rapid Development**: Django's built-in tools allow developers to focus on building the application rather than spending time on repetitive tasks such as authentication, database setup, and URL routing.

2. **Security**: Django places a strong emphasis on security, offering features like protection against SQL injection, cross-site scripting (XSS), and cross-site request forgery (CSRF). It also provides secure password handling and authentication mechanisms.

3. **Scalability**: Django is designed to scale well. It can be used to build everything from simple content management systems

(CMS) to complex social media platforms or e-commerce websites.

4. **Extensive Documentation**: Django has comprehensive and well-maintained documentation, making it easy for both beginners and professionals to dive into development.

5. **Community Support**: With an active and vibrant community, Django developers benefit from a wide range of third-party libraries, plugins, and packages that extend its functionality.

Overview of Django's MVT Architecture

Django follows a software design pattern called **Model-View-Template (MVT)**. While it's similar to the more widely known Model-View-Controller (MVC) pattern, the terminology differs slightly. Here's a breakdown of the MVT architecture in Django:

1. **Model**:

   - The model represents the data structure of your application. It defines the fields and behaviors of the data you're working with. In Django, models are Python classes that subclass django.db.models.Model.

   - Models interact with the database, performing actions such as creating, retrieving, updating, and deleting records.

2. **View**:

   - The view is responsible for the business logic of your application. It takes user input, interacts with the model to fetch or modify data, and passes it to the template for rendering.

o Views in Django are written as Python functions or class-based views (CBVs) and are mapped to specific URLs through Django's URL dispatcher.

3. Template:

o The template handles the presentation logic. It is responsible for rendering the HTML page that is sent to the user's browser. Django uses a templating language that allows you to embed Python-like expressions inside HTML to display dynamic data.

o Templates are HTML files with placeholders for data passed from the view.

Together, the MVT components enable Django to process requests, interact with the database, and render dynamic web pages in an efficient manner.

Setting Up a Django Project

Let's walk through setting up a Django project from scratch. We'll start by installing Django and creating a new project.

1. **Install Django**: If you haven't installed Django yet, you can do so using the following pip command:

bash

```
pip install django
```

2. **Create a Django Project**: Once Django is installed, you can create a new project using the django-admin command:

bash

```
django-admin startproject
myproject
```

This will create a new folder named myproject with the necessary Django project structure.

3. **Start the Development Server**: To ensure everything is working, navigate to the myproject folder and run the development server:

bash

```
cd myproject
python manage.py runserver
```

You should see a message telling you that the server is running. Open your browser and go to http://127.0.0.1:8000/—you should see the default Django welcome page!

3.2 Building a Simple Web App with Django

Creating Models, Views, and Templates

Now that you have your Django project set up, it's time to start building a simple web application. We'll create a basic blog app where users can view and create posts.

1. **Create a Django App**: Django projects consist of one or more apps. To create an app, use the following command:

```bash

python manage.py startapp blog
```

This will create a new folder called blog where we will store our models, views, and templates.

2. **Define the Model**: Models define the structure of the database tables. In our blog app, we'll create a Post model to represent blog posts.

Open blog/models.py and add the following code:

python

```
from django.db import models

class Post(models.Model):
    title =
models.CharField(max_length=100)
    content = models.TextField()
    created_at =
models.DateTimeField(auto_now_add=
True)
```

```python
def __str__(self):
    return self.title
```

- title: The title of the blog post.

- content: The content of the blog post.

- created_at: A timestamp that automatically records when the post was created.

3. **Create the Database Table**: Once you've defined the model, run the following commands to create the necessary database tables:

```
bash
```

```
python manage.py makemigrations
python manage.py migrate
```

4. **Create a View**: Now, we'll create a view to display all blog posts. In blog/views.py, add the following:

```python
from django.shortcuts import render
from .models import Post

def post_list(request):
    posts = Post.objects.all()
    return render(request, 'blog/post_list.html', {'posts': posts})
```

- ○ Post.objects.all(): This fetches all blog posts from the database.

- ○ render(): This renders the template post_list.html and passes the posts to it.

5. **Create a Template**: In Django, templates are stored in the templates folder. Create a folder named blog/templates/blog/ and add a file called post_list.html with the following content:

html

```html
<!DOCTYPE html>
<html>
<head>
    <title>Blog Posts</title>
</head>
<body>
    <h1>Blog Posts</h1>
    <ul>
        {% for post in posts %}
            <li>
                <h2>{{ post.title }}</h2>
```

```
                    <p>{{ post.content
}}</p>
                    <p><em>Created on:
{{ post.created_at }}</em></p>
            </li>
        {% endfor %}
    </ul>
</body>
</html>
```

- o This template iterates through the posts variable and displays the title, content, and creation date for each post.

6. **Map the View to a URL**: Now, we need to map our view to a URL. In blog/urls.py, add the following:

```python
from django.urls import path
from . import views
```

```
urlpatterns = [
    path('', views.post_list,
name='post_list'),
]
```

Then, include this **URL** configuration in your project's main urls.py (located in the myproject folder):

```python
from django.contrib import admin
from django.urls import path,
include

urlpatterns = [
    path('admin/',
admin.site.urls),
    path('',
include('blog.urls')),
]
```

7. **Run the Development Server**: Finally, run the development server again:

```bash
```

```
python manage.py runserver
```

Navigate to http://127.0.0.1:8000/ to see your blog posts displayed!

Implementing Database Operations with Django ORM

Django provides a powerful ORM (Object-Relational Mapping) to interact with the database without writing raw SQL. Here's how you can add, edit, and delete posts using Django ORM.

1. **Adding Posts**: You can add new posts either through the Django admin panel or by using Django's shell. To add a post via the shell, run:

```bash
```

```bash
python manage.py shell
```

In the shell, enter the following:

```python
```

```python
from blog.models import Post
post = Post(title='My First Post',
content='This is the content of
the first post.')
post.save()
```

2. **Editing Posts**: You can retrieve and edit posts like this:

```python
```

```python
post = Post.objects.get(id=1)   #
Get post with ID 1
post.title = 'Updated Title'
post.save()   # Save the changes to
the database
```

3. **Deleting Posts**: To delete a post:

python

```
post = Post.objects.get(id=1)
post.delete()
```

Setting Up Django Admin Interface

Django includes an automatically generated admin interface, where you can add, edit, and delete records from your database. To use it, follow these steps:

1. **Create a Superuser**: Run the following command to create a superuser account:

bash

```
python manage.py createsuperuser
```

Follow the prompts to set the username, email, and password.

2. **Register Your Models in the Admin**: Open blog/admin.py and register the Post model:

```python

from django.contrib import admin
from .models import Post

admin.site.register(Post)
```

3. **Access the Admin Panel**: Start the development server and visit http://127.0.0.1:8000/admin/. Log in using the superuser credentials you created. From here, you can manage your blog posts directly through the admin interface.

3.3 Django Authentication and Authorization

User Authentication: Login and Signup

Django provides built-in authentication features for handling user registration, login, and logout. Here's how to set up basic authentication:

1. **Setting Up Authentication Views**: In blog/urls.py, add the following:

```python
from django.urls import path
from django.contrib.auth import views as auth_views

urlpatterns = [
```

```
    path('login/',
auth_views.LoginView.as_view(),
name='login'),
    path('logout/',
auth_views.LogoutView.as_view(),
name='logout'),
    path('signup/', views.signup,
name='signup'),
]
```

2. **Creating a Signup View**: In views.py, add a simple view for signing up users:

python

```
from django.shortcuts import
render, redirect
from django.contrib.auth.forms
import UserCreationForm

def signup(request):
    if request.method == 'POST':
```

```
        form =
UserCreationForm(request.POST)
        if form.is_valid():
            form.save()
            return
redirect('login')
    else:
        form = UserCreationForm()
    return render(request,
'signup.html', {'form': form})
```

3. **Creating the Signup Template**: Create a signup.html template with a form:

```html
<form method="POST">
    {% csrf_token %}
    {{ form.as_p }}
    <button type="submit">Sign
Up</button>
</form>
```

4. **Run the Server**: Now, when you visit /signup/, you can create a new user account.

3.4 Deploying Django Applications

Preparing for Deployment

Before deploying your Django app, ensure that you've made the following preparations:

1. **Set the DEBUG Mode to False**: In settings.py, change DEBUG to False:

```python

DEBUG = False
```

2. **Configure Allowed Hosts**: Set the ALLOWED_HOSTS to include your domain name or IP address:

```python
```

```python
ALLOWED_HOSTS = ['yourdomain.com',
'127.0.0.1']
```

3. **Set Up Static and Media Files**: Configure Django to serve static files (CSS, JavaScript) and media files (images, uploads) during production.

Deploying Django to Heroku or DigitalOcean

1. **Deploying to Heroku:**

   o Install the Heroku CLI.

   o Create a Procfile in your project directory:

```makefile
web: gunicorn myproject.wsgi
```

o Install the required dependencies:

bash

```
pip install gunicorn dj-database-
url
```

o Commit your changes and push to Heroku:

bash

```
git push heroku master
```

2. **Deploying to DigitalOcean**: DigitalOcean provides cloud hosting where you can set up a virtual private server (VPS) for hosting your Django application. You can follow DigitalOcean's tutorials for Django deployment.

Conclusion

In this chapter, we explored Django, from setting up a project to building a simple web app. We also covered essential topics like user authentication and deployment. Django's simplicity, security, and scalability make it an ideal choice for building back-end applications, whether you're working on a small blog or a large e-commerce platform.

In the following chapters, we'll continue building upon this foundation and dive deeper into advanced Django topics.

Chapter 4: Exploring FastAPI for Fast, Modern APIs

4.1 Introduction to FastAPI

FastAPI vs Django: When to Use Each

When considering web frameworks for building APIs, Django and FastAPI are two of the most commonly discussed options. Both are powerful, but they serve different needs and excel in different scenarios. Let's break down when to use each framework.

1. **Django:**

- Django is a full-stack web framework that provides everything you need to build an application. It's built around the **Model-View-Template (MVT)** pattern and includes an ORM, authentication system, admin panel, and more.

- **Use Django** when you are building a full-stack application and need an all-in-one solution for everything from the database to user interfaces.

- It is ideal for projects with complex, relational database-driven applications where the back-end needs to integrate tightly with the front-end.

2. **FastAPI**:

- FastAPI is a lightweight web framework primarily designed for building high-performance, asynchronous APIs. It is built on top of Starlette (for the web parts) and Pydantic (for data validation). FastAPI focuses on building APIs that are not just fast but also easy to use, with automatic generation of API documentation (Swagger).

- **Use FastAPI** when you are building APIs that need to handle a high number of concurrent requests or require asynchronous programming. FastAPI is great for **microservices**, real-time applications (such as chat apps), or data-heavy applications (like machine learning APIs).

○ It's perfect for modern APIs that benefit from high speed and asynchronous capabilities.

So, if you're building a **full-stack web app** with a traditional database and need a lot of built-in tools, **Django** might be a better choice. However, if you're focused purely on creating a **fast, scalable, and asynchronous API**, **FastAPI** is the better option.

Features of FastAPI: Speed, Asynchronous Support

FastAPI is known for its impressive speed, not only in terms of response time but also for development time. Some key features that make FastAPI stand out are:

1. **Performance**:

- o FastAPI is one of the fastest web frameworks available. It leverages asynchronous capabilities via Python's asyncio to handle requests concurrently, making it ideal for building high-performance APIs that need to scale.

- o FastAPI is built on **Starlette**, a framework designed for speed and high concurrency. As a result, FastAPI can handle thousands of requests per second, making it one of the best frameworks for performance.

2. **Asynchronous Support:**

- o FastAPI is designed to be asynchronous from the ground up. This means it can handle many requests at the same time without blocking, which is ideal for applications like real-time messaging or APIs with long-running operations (e.g., connecting to external services, or processing large datasets).

3. **Automatic API Documentation:**

   o One of FastAPI's most standout features is **automatic interactive API documentation**. Using **Swagger UI** and **ReDoc**, FastAPI automatically generates documentation for the API that's easy to test and use, right out of the box.

4. **Type Checking and Validation with Pydantic:**

   o FastAPI uses **Pydantic**, which allows you to perform automatic validation and type checking on the incoming request data. It automatically converts data types (such as converting strings to integers) and ensures that the incoming data matches the expected schema.

Installing and Setting Up FastAPI

Let's set up a FastAPI application from scratch. Follow these steps:

1. **Installing FastAPI and Uvicorn**: FastAPI itself is lightweight, but it requires an ASGI server to run. **Uvicorn** is a great option for this. To install FastAPI and Uvicorn, run the following command:

```bash
bash
```

```bash
pip install fastapi uvicorn
```

2. **Creating a FastAPI App**: Now that FastAPI and Uvicorn are installed, let's create our first API. Create a new Python file, say main.py, and add the following code:

```python
from fastapi import FastAPI

app = FastAPI()

@app.get("/")
def read_root():
    return {"message": "Hello, World!"}
```

This creates a FastAPI application with a single endpoint (/) that returns a JSON message.

3. **Running the Server**: To run the FastAPI app, use Uvicorn as the ASGI server. In the terminal, run:

```bash
uvicorn main:app --reload
```

The --reload flag ensures that the server reloads automatically whenever you make changes to the code.

4. **Testing the API**: Now, open your browser and navigate to http://127.0.0.1:8000/. You should see the message:

```json
{"message": "Hello, World!"}
```

FastAPI also automatically generates API documentation for your app. Go to http://127.0.0.1:8000/docs to see an interactive API documentation page powered by **Swagger UI**.

4.2 Creating and Handling APIs with FastAPI

Building a Simple CRUD API

Let's build a simple **CRUD (Create, Read, Update, Delete)** API using FastAPI to manage a list of items.

1. **Defining the Item Model**: We'll start by defining an Item model that will represent our items in the API. FastAPI uses **Pydantic models** to define data schemas. Create a new file models.py:

python

```python
from pydantic import BaseModel

class Item(BaseModel):
    name: str
    description: str
```

```
price: float
tax: float = None
```

- o BaseModel: Pydantic's base class that allows automatic data validation.

2. **Creating CRUD Operations**: Now let's create the API to handle basic CRUD operations. Add the following to main.py:

python

```python
from fastapi import FastAPI
from models import Item
from typing import List

app = FastAPI()

fake_items_db = {}

@app.post("/items/",
response_model=Item)
def create_item(item: Item):
```

```python
    fake_items_db[item.name] =
item
    return item


@app.get("/items/{item_name}",
response_model=Item)
def read_item(item_name: str):
    return
fake_items_db.get(item_name)


@app.put("/items/{item_name}",
response_model=Item)
def update_item(item_name: str,
item: Item):
    fake_items_db[item_name] =
item
    return item


@app.delete("/items/{item_name}")
def delete_item(item_name: str):
    if item_name in fake_items_db:
```

```
        del
fake_items_db[item_name]
        return {"message": f"Item
{item_name} deleted"}
    return {"error": "Item not
found"}
```

- o @app.post(): Used to create a new item.

- o @app.get(): Fetches the item based on its name.

- o @app.put(): Updates an existing item.

- o @app.delete(): Deletes an item by name.

3. **Testing the CRUD API**: Run the FastAPI application again with uvicorn and navigate to http://127.0.0.1:8000/docs to test the CRUD operations via Swagger UI.

Working with Data Validation and Pydantic Models

FastAPI uses Pydantic models for request validation. Here's how it works:

1. **Automatic Data Validation**: When you define a Pydantic model like Item, FastAPI automatically validates incoming request data. If the incoming data doesn't match the model (e.g., if the price is missing or a non-float value is provided), FastAPI will return a 422 Unprocessable Entity error along with the validation error message.

2. **Optional Fields and Default Values**: You can set default values in your Pydantic models. For example, the tax field in the Item model is optional because we've set a default value of None.

Handling Requests and Responses with FastAPI

FastAPI makes it easy to handle incoming requests and format responses. Here's how:

1. **Request Parameters**: You can easily accept query parameters in the request URL:

python

```python
@app.get("/items/")
def get_items(skip: int = 0,
limit: int = 10):
    return {"skip": skip, "limit":
limit}
```

FastAPI will automatically map the query parameters to the function arguments. For example, accessing http://127.0.0.1:8000/items/?skip=0&limit=5 would return:

```json
{"skip": 0, "limit": 5}
```

2. **Response Models**: You can specify a response model for FastAPI to serialize the response:

```python
@app.get("/items/{item_name}",
response_model=Item)
def get_item(item_name: str):
    return
fake_items_db.get(item_name)
```

FastAPI automatically serializes the Python data into JSON, and uses the response model to ensure that the data matches the expected structure.

4.3 Asynchronous Programming with FastAPI

Understanding Asynchronous Programming

Asynchronous programming is a technique that allows you to write code that doesn't block the execution of other tasks. This is particularly useful for handling I/O-bound operations, such as:

- Fetching data from external APIs.

- Reading/writing files.

- Querying a database.

With asynchronous programming, FastAPI can handle multiple requests concurrently, without waiting for one operation to complete before starting another.

Building Asynchronous Routes

To build asynchronous routes in FastAPI, you simply define the route handler with the async def syntax:

python

```python
@app.get("/items/{item_name}")
async def get_item(item_name: str):
    # Simulating a long-running I/O operation
    await some_async_function()
    return {"item": item_name}
```

The await keyword is used to indicate that the function should wait for the result of an asynchronous operation before proceeding.

Async with Databases and External APIs

1. **Async with Databases**: FastAPI can be used with asynchronous databases like **Databases** or **SQLAlchemy** with async support to fetch and modify data asynchronously.

2. **Async with External APIs**: If your API needs to call an external API, you can use httpx (an async HTTP client) to perform asynchronous HTTP requests:

```python
import httpx

async def fetch_data():
    async with httpx.AsyncClient() as client:
```

```
    response = await
client.get('https://api.example.co
m/data')
    return response.json()
```

4.4 FastAPI Authentication and Security

Implementing JWT Authentication

JSON Web Tokens (JWT) are commonly used for authentication in modern web applications. FastAPI makes it easy to implement JWT-based authentication.

1. **Install Required Libraries**:

bash

```
pip install pyjwt
```

2. **Create the JWT Token**: You can create a JWT token using the pyjwt library:

```python

import jwt
from datetime import datetime,
timedelta

SECRET_KEY = "your_secret_key"
ALGORITHM = "HS256"

def create_access_token(data:
dict):
    expiration = datetime.utcnow()
+ timedelta(hours=1)
    to_encode = data.()
    to_encode.update({"exp":
expiration})
    return jwt.encode(to_encode,
SECRET_KEY, algorithm=ALGORITHM)
```

3. **Verify the JWT Token**: You can verify the token on incoming requests by using a dependency that decodes the JWT:

[101]

```python

from fastapi import Depends,
HTTPException, status
from fastapi.security import
OAuth2PasswordBearer

oauth2_scheme =
OAuth2PasswordBearer(tokenUrl="tok
en")

def get_current_user(token: str =
Depends(oauth2_scheme)):
    try:
        payload =
jwt.decode(token, SECRET_KEY,
algorithms=[ALGORITHM])
        return payload
    except
jwt.ExpiredSignatureError:
```

```
        raise
HTTPException(status_code=status.H
TTP_401_UNAUTHORIZED,
detail="Token expired")
    except jwt.JWTError:
        raise
HTTPException(status_code=status.H
TTP_401_UNAUTHORIZED,
detail="Token invalid")
```

OAuth2 Integration for External Login

You can integrate **OAuth2** authentication (such as login via Google or Facebook) using the OAuth2PasswordBearer and external libraries like **Authlib** or **python-social-auth**.

[103]

Conclusion

In this chapter, we've explored the power of FastAPI—its performance, ease of use, and features like asynchronous support, automatic validation, and detailed API documentation. We've also built a simple CRUD API, implemented JWT authentication, and explored how to handle asynchronous operations effectively.

With FastAPI, you can easily build high-performance APIs, scale them, and secure them with robust authentication methods. Whether you're building a small microservice or a large application, FastAPI offers the tools and speed to get the job done efficiently.

Chapter 5: Front-End Development with React

5.1 Introduction to React

What is React and Why Use It?

React is a popular JavaScript library for building user interfaces, particularly for single-page applications (SPAs). It was developed by Facebook and has since become one of the most widely used front-end libraries for web development. But what makes React stand out from other JavaScript frameworks?

1. **Declarative UI**: React allows you to describe how the user interface (UI) should look based on the state of your application. Instead of directly manipulating the DOM,

you describe the components in terms of their state, and React takes care of updating the UI efficiently.

2. **Component-Based Architecture**: In React, everything is a component. A component is a reusable piece of code that represents a part of the UI. Components can be as small as a button or as large as a page, and they can be composed together to build complex UIs.

3. **Virtual DOM**: React uses a virtual DOM, which is a lightweight of the actual DOM. When state changes in your application, React updates the virtual DOM first, compares it to the real DOM, and then only makes the necessary changes. This minimizes direct DOM manipulation and optimizes performance.

4. **Reusable Components**: Components are reusable, meaning that once you create a component, you can use it in multiple places. This leads to less code duplication and a more modular architecture.

5. **Unidirectional Data Flow**: React uses a one-way data flow, meaning data always flows from parent to child components. This makes the flow of data easier to manage and debug, especially in large applications.

React is highly regarded for its simplicity, flexibility, and performance. Whether you're building a simple interactive UI or a complex single-page application, React provides the tools you need to create fast and dynamic user interfaces.

React Components and JSX

At the heart of React are **components**. Components are the building blocks of a React application, and they define how a part of the user interface should look and behave. There are two types of components in React:

1. **Functional Components**: These are simply JavaScript functions that return JSX (more on that below). They are the most common type of component in modern React development.

2. **Class Components**: Class components were the original type of component in React. They use ES6 class syntax and require the use of lifecycle methods for state and side effects. However, with the advent of React Hooks, functional components have become more popular because they are simpler and easier to work with.

JSX (JavaScript XML) is a syntax extension for JavaScript that allows you to write HTML-like code within JavaScript. JSX is used to define the UI structure in React components. React will convert JSX into JavaScript code that the browser can understand.

Here's an example of a simple functional component using JSX:

```
javascript
```

```
import React from 'react';

function Greeting(props) {
  return <h1>Hello,
{props.name}!</h1>;
}

export default Greeting;
```

In the example above:

- Greeting is a functional component that accepts props as an argument and returns JSX. The props object contains any data passed to the component when it is used, such as the name value in this case.

- The JSX <h1>Hello, {props.name}!</h1> gets transformed into a JavaScript function call that renders an HTML h1 element.

Setting Up a React Development Environment

To get started with React, you need to set up your development environment. The easiest way to do this is by using **Create React App**, a tool that sets up everything for you automatically.

1. **Install Node.js**: React relies on **Node.js** and **npm** (Node Package Manager). First, make sure Node.js is installed on your machine. You can download it from nodejs.org.

2. **Install Create React App**: To create a new React application, you can use the Create React App command-line tool:

```bash
```

```bash
npx create-react-app my-app
cd my-app
```

3. **Start the Development Server**: After the installation is complete, you can start the development server:

```bash
```

```bash
npm start
```

This will open your new React app in the browser at http://localhost:3000/.

Now, you have everything set up and ready to start building React components.

5.2 Understanding React State and Props

Managing State in Functional Components

State is one of the most important concepts in React. It allows components to maintain information between renders. When state changes, React re-renders the component to reflect the updated state in the UI.

In **functional components**, state is managed using a Hook called useState. Here's how you can use it:

1. **Using useState**: The useState Hook is used to create state variables inside a functional component. It returns two values: the current state value and a function to update that value.

Example:

```javascript
import React, { useState } from
'react';

function Counter() {
  const [count, setCount] =
useState(0);

  return (
    <div>
      <h1>Count: {count}</h1>
      <button onClick={() =>
setCount(count +
1)}>Increment</button>
    </div>
  );
}

export default Counter;
```

In the example above:

- useState(0) initializes the count state variable to 0.

- setCount(count + 1) is called whenever the button is clicked, updating the count value and re-rendering the component.

2. **Handling Complex State**: For more complex state, you can use objects or arrays. When using an object or array, you can update a specific property or element without overwriting the entire state.

Example:

```javascript
const [user, setUser] = useState({ name: 'John', age: 30 });
```

```javascript
const updateName = () => {
  setUser((prevUser) => ({
...prevUser, name: 'Alice' }));
};
```

Using Props to Pass Data Between Components

Props (short for "properties") allow you to pass data from one component to another. In React, data always flows **from parent to child** components.

Example of using props:

```javascript
javascript


import React from 'react';


function Parent() {
  const name = 'Alice';

  return <Child name={name} />;
```

```
}

function Child(props) {
  return <h1>Hello,
{props.name}!</h1>;
}

export default Parent;
```

In this example:

- Parent passes the name prop to Child.

- Child receives the name prop and renders it in the UI.

Props can be any type of data—strings, numbers, arrays, objects, or even functions.

Handling User Input with Forms

Handling forms in React involves managing state for input fields. Here's how you can handle user input with a form:

1. **Creating a Controlled Component:** A controlled component is one where React manages the value of the input field.

Example:

```javascript
function MyForm() {
  const [inputValue,
setInputValue] = useState('');

  const handleChange = (event) =>
{

setInputValue(event.target.value);
  };

  const handleSubmit = (event) =>
{
    event.preventDefault();
```

```
    alert('Form submitted with
input: ' + inputValue);
  };


  return (
    <form onSubmit={handleSubmit}>
      <input
        type="text"
        value={inputValue}
        onChange={handleChange}
      />
      <button
type="submit">Submit</button>
    </form>
  );
}


export default MyForm;
```

In this example:

- o The inputValue state variable holds the current value of the input field.

- o handleChange updates the state whenever the user types in the field.

- o handleSubmit prevents the default form submission behavior and shows an alert with the current input value.

5.3 Component Lifecycle in React

Understanding Component Mounting and Unmounting

In class components, lifecycle methods like componentDidMount and componentWillUnmount allow developers to run code at specific points during the component's lifecycle. In functional components, React provides **Hooks** that replicate these lifecycle methods.

1. **useEffect Hook**: The useEffect hook is used to perform side effects in functional components, such as fetching data, subscribing to events, or manually manipulating the DOM. It replaces lifecycle methods like componentDidMount and componentWillUnmount.

Example of useEffect for mounting:

```javascript
import React, { useState,
useEffect } from 'react';

function App() {
  const [data, setData] =
useState(null);
```

```
  useEffect(() => {

fetch('https://api.example.com/dat
a')
      .then((response) =>
response.json())
      .then((data) =>
setData(data));
  }, []); // Empty array means
this effect runs only once (on
mount)

  return <div>{data ?
JSON.stringify(data) :
'Loading...'}</div>;
}

export default App;
```

- useEffect is called after the component is mounted, and it fetches data from an API.

- The empty array [] means the effect will only run once (like componentDidMount in class components).

2. **Cleaning Up with useEffect**: If your effect involves resources like event listeners or timers, you can clean them up using the return function inside useEffect.

Example of cleanup:

```javascript
useEffect(() => {
  const timer = setInterval(() =>
console.log('Tick'), 1000);
```

```
    return () =>
clearInterval(timer); // Cleanup
on unmount
}, []);
```

Optimizing Performance with Memoization

1. **React.memo**: React.memo is a higher-order component that memoizes a component, preventing unnecessary re-renders when props haven't changed.

Example:

```javascript
const MyComponent =
React.memo(function
MyComponent(props) {
  return <div>{props.name}</div>;
});
```

- React.memo ensures that MyComponent only re-renders if the props.name value changes.

2. **useMemo**: useMemo is a Hook that memoizes values. It's useful for expensive computations that you only want to recalculate when certain dependencies change.

Example:

javascript

```
const memoizedValue = useMemo(()
=> expensiveFunction(data),
[data]);
```

5.4 React Router for Navigation

Introduction to React Router

React Router is a standard library for routing in React applications. It allows you to navigate between different components, simulate multi-page navigation in single-page applications, and manage URLs in a dynamic way.

1. **Installing React Router**: First, install the React Router library:

bash

```
npm install react-router-dom
```

2. **Setting Up Basic Routing**: Import BrowserRouter, Route, and Switch from react-router-dom to set up routes.

Example:

javascript

```
import { BrowserRouter as Router,
Route, Switch } from 'react-
router-dom';

function App() {
  return (
    <Router>
      <nav>
        <ul>
          <li><Link
to="/">Home</Link></li>
          <li><Link
to="/about">About</Link></li>
        </ul>
      </nav>

      <Switch>
        <Route path="/" exact>
          <Home />
        </Route>
        <Route path="/about">
```

```
        <About />
      </Route>
    </Switch>
  </Router>
  );
}
```

```
export default App;
```

Handling Dynamic Routing

React Router allows you to create dynamic routes that respond to parameters in the URL.

Example:

```javascript
```

```
<Route path="/user/:id"
component={User} />
```

The :id part of the route is a **dynamic segment,** and you can access it in the component via useParams().

Creating Nested Routes and Redirects

You can also create nested routes and handle redirects using React Router.

Example of nested routes:

```javascript
<Route path="/profile"
component={Profile}>
    <Route path="settings"
component={Settings} />
</Route>
```

Example of a redirect:

```javascript
import { Redirect } from 'react-router-dom';

<Redirect to="/login" />
```

Conclusion

In this chapter, we covered the fundamentals of front-end development with React. We explored how to create functional components, manage state and props, understand component lifecycles, and implement routing with React Router. React provides a powerful, efficient, and flexible way to build interactive UIs, making it a fantastic choice for modern web development. Whether you're building a small app or a large-scale project, React offers the tools you need to create dynamic, engaging user interfaces.

Chapter 6: Connecting React with Django and FastAPI

6.1 Understanding the Full-Stack Workflow

How React Communicates with Django/FastAPI

When building a full-stack application, React, Django, and FastAPI are often used together to create the front-end and back-end parts of the application. React handles the user interface and interactions, while Django or FastAPI serves as the back-end, handling business logic, database operations, and API requests.

React and Django/FastAPI Communication happens through **HTTP requests**. The front-end sends requests (usually via RESTful APIs) to the back-end, and the back-end responds with data. Here's a basic workflow of how this communication typically happens:

1. **React (Front-End)**: Sends requests (e.g., GET, POST, PUT, DELETE) to the back-end.

2. **Django/FastAPI (Back-End)**: The back-end processes the request, interacts with the database if needed, and returns a response (usually in JSON format).

3. **React (Front-End)**: React receives the response and updates the user interface based on the data.

This approach allows the front-end and back-end to be developed independently and communicate over a network (often using **RESTful APIs**).

Overview of RESTful APIs and JSON

A **RESTful API** (Representational State Transfer) is an architectural style that uses HTTP requests to access and manipulate resources (data). These resources are represented as URLs and interact with standard HTTP methods like **GET**, **POST**, **PUT**, and **DELETE**.

- **GET**: Retrieves data from the server.

- **POST**: Sends data to the server (usually to create a new resource).

- **PUT**: Updates an existing resource on the server.

- **DELETE**: Removes a resource from the server.

JSON (JavaScript Object Notation) is a lightweight data-interchange format that is easy for humans to read and write, and easy for machines to parse and generate. It's commonly used for transmitting data between a server and a client in web applications.

Example of a JSON response:

```json
{
  "id": 1,
  "name": "John Doe",
```

```
"email": "john@example.com"
}
```

Setting Up React to Call API Endpoints

To connect React with a Django or FastAPI back-end, we use HTTP requests. In React, this can be done using **fetch()** or **Axios**, two common methods for making requests.

Step 1: Setting Up the Backend

Let's assume you have a back-end API set up with Django or FastAPI. Here's an example of how you might define a basic **GET** endpoint in each:

- **Django**: In your views.py, you might have something like this:

```python
from django.http import JsonResponse
```

```python
def get_user(request):
    user_data = {"id": 1, "name":
"John Doe", "email":
"john@example.com"}
    return JsonResponse(user_data)
```

- **FastAPI**: In main.py, you could have:

python

```python
from fastapi import FastAPI


app = FastAPI()


@app.get("/user")
def get_user():
    return {"id": 1, "name": "John
Doe", "email": "john@example.com"}
```

Step 2: Fetching Data in React

In React, you can use **fetch()** or **Axios** to request data from these API endpoints. Here's an example using **fetch()**:

```javascript

import React, { useEffect,
useState } from 'react';

function User() {
  const [user, setUser] =
useState(null);

  useEffect(() => {

fetch('http://localhost:8000/user'
) // URL of your API
      .then(response =>
response.json())
      .then(data => setUser(data))
```

```
      .catch(error =>
console.error('Error fetching
data:', error));
  }, []);

  if (!user) return
<div>Loading...</div>;

  return (
    <div>
      <h1>{user.name}</h1>
      <p>Email: {user.email}</p>
    </div>
  );
}


export default User;
```

In the above code:

- We use the useEffect hook to fetch data when the component mounts.

- fetch() is used to make the GET request to the API, and the response is converted to JSON and stored in the user state.

- Once the data is fetched, the user information is displayed.

6.2 Fetching Data from Django API

Using fetch() and Axios to Make HTTP Requests

React allows you to fetch data from external APIs using various methods. Two common methods are **fetch()** and **Axios**.

Using fetch()

fetch() is a built-in JavaScript function that makes HTTP requests. It's a simple and lightweight way to get data from an API.

Example:

javascript

```
fetch('http://localhost:8000/user'
)
  .then(response =>
response.json())
  .then(data => {
    console.log(data);
  })
  .catch(error => {
    console.error('Error:',
error);
  });
```

Using Axios

Axios is a promise-based HTTP client that simplifies making requests and handling responses. It is more feature-rich than fetch(), with automatic **JSON** parsing, request/response interceptors, and more.

To use Axios, first install it:

bash

```
npm install axios
```

Example:

javascript

```
import axios from 'axios';

axios.get('http://localhost:8000/user')
  .then(response => {
    console.log(response.data);
  })
  .catch(error => {
    console.error('Error fetching data:', error);
  });
```

Handling API Responses and Updating State

After fetching data from an API, you typically need to update the component's state. In React, this is done using the useState hook.

Example with **Axios**:

```javascript

import React, { useEffect, useState } from 'react';
import axios from 'axios';

function User() {
  const [user, setUser] =
useState(null);

  useEffect(() => {
```

```
axios.get('http://localhost:8000/u
ser')
      .then(response => {
        setUser(response.data);
      })
      .catch(error => {
        console.error('Error
fetching data:', error);
      });
  }, []);

  if (!user) return
<div>Loading...</div>;

  return (
    <div>
      <h1>{user.name}</h1>
      <p>Email: {user.email}</p>
    </div>
  );
```

```
}
```

```
export default User;
```

Here, when the component mounts, the useEffect hook triggers the HTTP request. The response is stored in the user state using the setUser function, and the component re-renders to display the data.

Displaying Data in React Components

Once the data is fetched and stored in state, you can display it in your React components just like any other state variable.

```javascript

return (
  <div>
    <h1>{user.name}</h1>
    <p>Email: {user.email}</p>
```

```
    </div>
);
```

This dynamic rendering ensures that your UI updates as new data is fetched, providing a smooth and responsive experience for the user.

6.3 Implementing Authentication in Full-Stack Apps

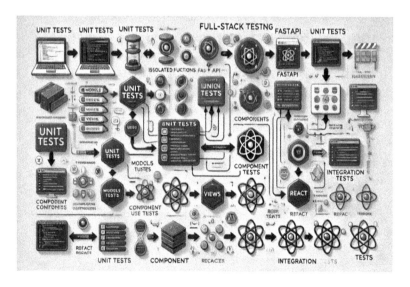

Managing JWT Tokens Between Django/FastAPI and React

Authentication is a critical aspect of full-stack applications. **JWT (JSON Web Tokens)** is a popular method of handling authentication in modern web applications. It allows users to securely authenticate with the back-end and maintain their session without constantly sending credentials.

Here's how to implement JWT authentication between React and Django/FastAPI:

Step 1: Back-End Setup

Both **Django** and **FastAPI** can be configured to issue JWT tokens after successful authentication. Here's how you can set it up:

- **Django**: You can use the djangorestframework-simplejwt package to handle JWTs in Django. After the user logs in, the server will issue a JWT that the client will store and send with future requests.

Example using djangorestframework-simplejwt:

python

```
from
rest_framework_simplejwt.views
import TokenObtainPairView,
TokenRefreshView

urlpatterns = [
    path('api/token/',
TokenObtainPairView.as_view(),
name='token_obtain_pair'),
    path('api/token/refresh/',
TokenRefreshView.as_view(),
name='token_refresh'),
]
```

- **FastAPI**: FastAPI has built-in support for JWT authentication using the OAuth2PasswordBearer and JWT libraries.

Example:

python

```python
from fastapi import FastAPI,
Depends, HTTPException
from fastapi.security import
OAuth2PasswordBearer
from jose import JWTError, jwt

oauth2_scheme =
OAuth2PasswordBearer(tokenUrl="tok
en")

def get_current_user(token: str =
Depends(oauth2_scheme)):
```

```
# Verify the JWT token and
return the current user
    pass
```

Step 2: Storing JWT in React

Once the user is authenticated, the server will return a JWT token. This token should be stored in **localStorage** or **sessionStorage** on the client-side. This allows the token to be sent with subsequent requests.

Example:

```
javascript
```

```
localStorage.setItem('token',
token);
```

Step 3: Sending JWT with Requests

After storing the JWT, you need to include it in the Authorization header of your HTTP requests. You can do this using either **fetch()** or **Axios**.

- **Using fetch():**

javascript

```javascript
fetch('http://localhost:8000/prote
cted', {
  method: 'GET',
  headers: {
    'Authorization': `Bearer
${localStorage.getItem('token')}`,
  }
})
```

- **Using Axios:**

javascript

```javascript
axios.get('http://localhost:8000/p
rotected', {
  headers: {
    Authorization: `Bearer
${localStorage.getItem('token')}`,
  }
```

```
})
```

Creating Protected Routes in React

To protect certain routes in React (i.e., to only allow authenticated users to access them), you can create **protected routes** that check whether a valid JWT exists.

Example:

```javascript
import React from 'react';
import { Redirect, Route } from
'react-router-dom';

function ProtectedRoute({
component: Component, ...rest }) {
  const isAuthenticated =
localStorage.getItem('token');
  return (
    <Route
```

```
    {...rest}
    render={(props) =>
      isAuthenticated ? (
        <Component {...props} />
      ) : (
        <Redirect to="/login" />
      )
    }
  />
);
}


export default ProtectedRoute;
```

Securing API Endpoints in Django/FastAPI

To secure your API endpoints, you must verify the JWT sent by the client in the request header. Here's how to do it:

- **Django**: In Django, you can use the SimpleJWT package to verify the token on the back-end.

Example:

python

```
from
rest_framework_simplejwt.authentic
ation import JWTAuthentication

class MyView(APIView):
    authentication_classes =
[JWTAuthentication]
    permission_classes =
[IsAuthenticated]

    def get(self, request):
        return
Response({"message": "You are
authenticated!"})
```

- **FastAPI**: FastAPI makes it easy to verify JWT tokens with the built-in dependencies system.

Example:

python

```python
from fastapi import Depends,
HTTPException
from fastapi.security import
OAuth2PasswordBearer
from jose import JWTError, jwt

def get_current_user(token: str =
Depends(oauth2_scheme)):
    try:
        payload =
jwt.decode(token, SECRET_KEY,
algorithms=[ALGORITHM])
        return payload
    except JWTError:
```

```
raise
HTTPException(status_code=401,
detail="Invalid token")
```

Conclusion

In this chapter, we explored how React can be connected to back-end APIs built with Django and FastAPI. We discussed how React communicates with these back-end services using **HTTP requests**, handling **API responses**, and updating the UI accordingly. Additionally, we covered **authentication** techniques using **JWT tokens**, including how to manage JWT tokens in React, create protected routes, and secure your API endpoints.

With this knowledge, you can create full-stack applications with a React front-end and Django/FastAPI back-end, ensuring smooth communication between the two while also securing user data and interactions.

Chapter 7: Working with Databases in Full-Stack Development

7.1 Introduction to Databases for Full-Stack Web Apps

SQL vs NoSQL: When to Use Each

Databases are the backbone of most web applications, and understanding the differences between **SQL** and **NoSQL** databases is crucial for building effective full-stack applications.

- **SQL (Structured Query Language) Databases**: These databases are **relational**, meaning data is stored in tables that have predefined schemas (columns with specific data types). SQL databases are ideal for structured data with relationships between entities. **PostgreSQL** and **MySQL** are examples of SQL databases.

- o **When to use SQL:**
  - You need a **structured data model** with complex relationships (e.g., customer orders in an e-commerce platform).
  - Your application needs to perform **complex queries** (e.g., joins, groupings, aggregations).
  - You require **ACID compliance** for transactions to ensure data integrity.

- **NoSQL (Not Only SQL) Databases:** These databases are **non-relational** and store data in formats like documents, key-value pairs, or graphs. They offer more flexibility when it comes to schema design and can handle unstructured or semi-structured data. **MongoDB** and **Cassandra** are popular NoSQL databases.

- **When to use NoSQL:**

  - You need a **flexible schema** (e.g., handling JSON documents that may change over time).

  - Your application requires **horizontal scaling** and high availability.

  - The data doesn't have complex relationships, or you need to handle large amounts of data (e.g., social media platforms, real-time analytics).

Understanding Relational Databases: PostgreSQL, MySQL

Relational databases (SQL databases) store data in **tables**, where each table consists of rows and columns. Each row represents a record, and each column represents a data attribute.

- **PostgreSQL**:
  - PostgreSQL is a powerful, open-source relational database system that supports advanced SQL queries, indexing, and ACID compliance.
  - It's ideal for applications that need to handle complex queries, data integrity, and transactional consistency.

Example of a simple **PostgreSQL** table definition:

```sql
CREATE TABLE users (
    id SERIAL PRIMARY KEY,
    username VARCHAR(100) NOT NULL,
    email VARCHAR(100) UNIQUE,
    created_at TIMESTAMP DEFAULT CURRENT_TIMESTAMP
);
```

- **MySQL**:

  o **MySQL** is another widely-used relational database management system (**RDBMS**), known for its speed and reliability.

- o It's suitable for applications that require structured data storage with a straightforward relational model.

Example of a simple **MySQL** table definition:

```sql
sql

CREATE TABLE users (
    id INT AUTO_INCREMENT PRIMARY KEY,
    username VARCHAR(100) NOT NULL,
    email VARCHAR(100) UNIQUE,
    created_at TIMESTAMP DEFAULT CURRENT_TIMESTAMP
);
```

Setting Up Database Connections in Django and FastAPI

To connect a database with your web application, you need to configure database connections properly. Let's look at how to set up database connections in both **Django** and **FastAPI**.

Django Database Connection

Django uses an ORM (Object-Relational Mapping) system to interact with databases. In your Django project's settings.py, you configure the database connection:

python

```python
DATABASES = {
    'default': {
        'ENGINE':
'django.db.backends.postgresql',
        'NAME': 'mydatabase',
        'USER': 'myuser',
        'PASSWORD': 'mypassword',
        'HOST': 'localhost',
        'PORT': '5432',
    }
```

```
}
```

Here:

- ENGINE specifies the database backend (PostgreSQL in this case).

- NAME, USER, PASSWORD, HOST, and PORT are your database credentials and connection settings.

After setting this up, Django automatically manages the connection for you when you run database queries.

FastAPI Database Connection with SQLAlchemy

FastAPI doesn't have a built-in ORM like Django, but you can use **SQLAlchemy** to manage database interactions. First, install SQLAlchemy:

bash

```bash
pip install sqlalchemy psycopg2
```

Then, create a file database.py to set up the database connection:

```python

from sqlalchemy import create_engine
from sqlalchemy.ext.declarative import declarative_base
from sqlalchemy.orm import sessionmaker

SQLALCHEMY_DATABASE_URL = "postgresql://myuser:mypassword@localhost/mydatabase"

engine = create_engine(SQLALCHEMY_DATABASE_URL, connect_args={"check_same_thread": False})
```

```
SessionLocal =
sessionmaker(autocommit=False,
autoflush=False, bind=engine)

Base = declarative_base()
```

Here:

- create_engine() creates a connection to the PostgreSQL database.

- SessionLocal() is the session factory used to interact with the database.

- Base is the base class for our ORM models.

Now you can use **SQLAlchemy** to define models and interact with the database.

7.2 Using Django ORM for Database Operations

Creating and Managing Models in Django

In Django, models are Python classes that define the structure of your database tables. Django automatically generates SQL to create tables and manages the relationships between them.

Here's how you create a simple User model in Django:

```python

from django.db import models

class User(models.Model):
    username =
models.CharField(max_length=100)
```

```
    email =
models.EmailField(unique=True)
    created_at =
models.DateTimeField(auto_now_add=
True)


    def __str__(self):
        return self.username
```

In this example:

- CharField is used for text fields.

- EmailField is a specialized field for email addresses.

- DateTimeField is used to store timestamps, with auto_now_add=True automatically setting the field to the current time when a new record is created.

Database Migrations with Django

After defining or modifying models in Django, you need to create and apply database migrations.

Migrations are used to update the database schema.

1. **Create Migrations**:

bash

```
python manage.py makemigrations
```

2. **Apply Migrations**:

bash

```
python manage.py migrate
```

Django will automatically apply the necessary changes to the database based on your models.

Querying and Filtering Data with Django ORM

Django provides a powerful ORM that allows you to query the database without writing raw SQL. Here are a few examples of common database queries in Django:

- **Retrieve all users:**

python

```
users = User.objects.all()
```

- **Filter users by a specific field:**

python

```
users =
User.objects.filter(username='john
_doe')
```

- **Get a single user by ID:**

python

```
user = User.objects.get(id=1)
```

- **Ordering results:**

python

```
users =
User.objects.order_by('created_at'
)
```

Django ORM supports advanced queries, like **aggregates**, **joins**, and **annotations**, that can be easily incorporated into your application.

7.3 Integrating FastAPI with Databases

Using SQLAlchemy with FastAPI

While Django has its own ORM, FastAPI relies on external libraries like **SQLAlchemy** for database interaction. Let's see how we can integrate **SQLAlchemy** with FastAPI to manage database operations.

Defining Models with SQLAlchemy

Here's an example of how to define a User model in FastAPI using SQLAlchemy:

```python
from sqlalchemy import Column,
Integer, String, DateTime
from sqlalchemy.ext.declarative
import declarative_base
from sqlalchemy.orm import
relationship
from datetime import datetime

Base = declarative_base()

class User(Base):
    __tablename__ = 'users'

    id = Column(Integer,
primary_key=True, index=True)
```

```
    username = Column(String,
index=True)
    email = Column(String,
unique=True, index=True)
    created_at = Column(DateTime,
default=datetime.utcnow)
```

In this example:

- Column() defines columns in the database table.

- primary_key=True makes the id field the primary key.

- index=True creates an index on the column for faster lookups.

- default=datetime.utcnow sets the default value of created_at to the current timestamp.

Creating the Database Session in FastAPI

Next, you need to create a session to interact with the database. We already defined the session in database.py earlier. Let's move on to writing CRUD operations.

Writing Async Database Queries

FastAPI supports **asynchronous programming**, which allows for non-blocking database queries. Here's an example of how to query the database asynchronously using SQLAlchemy and **Databases** (an async database library for SQLAlchemy):

1. **Install Databases:**

bash

pip install databases

2. **Async Session Setup:**

```python
python

import databases
import sqlalchemy
from sqlalchemy import
create_engine
from sqlalchemy.orm import
sessionmaker

DATABASE_URL =
"postgresql://myuser:mypassword@lo
calhost/mydatabase"
database =
databases.Database(DATABASE_URL)
engine =
create_engine(DATABASE_URL)
SessionLocal =
sessionmaker(autocommit=False,
autoflush=False, bind=engine)
```

3. Async CRUD Operations:

```python
python
```

```python
from fastapi import Depends,
HTTPException
from sqlalchemy.orm import Session


async def get_user_by_id(db:
Session, user_id: int):
    query =
db.query(User).filter(User.id ==
user_id)
    return query.first()


async def create_user(db: Session,
username: str, email: str):
    db_user =
User(username=username,
email=email)
    db.add(db_user)
    db.commit()
    db.refresh(db_user)
    return db_user
```

These async functions allow non-blocking queries to the database, which is useful when handling multiple requests simultaneously.

Handling Relationships and Foreign Keys

In relational databases, you often need to define relationships between tables. SQLAlchemy allows you to create relationships between models easily.

For example, a **one-to-many** relationship between User and Post could be defined as:

python

```python
class Post(Base):
    __tablename__ = 'posts'

    id = Column(Integer, primary_key=True, index=True)
```

```python
    title = Column(String,
index=True)
    content = Column(String)
    user_id = Column(Integer,
ForeignKey('users.id'))

    user = relationship('User',
back_populates='posts')

class User(Base):
    __tablename__ = 'users'

    id = Column(Integer,
primary_key=True, index=True)
    username = Column(String,
unique=True, index=True)
    posts = relationship('Post',
back_populates='user')
```
Here:

- ForeignKey establishes a relationship between the Post and User tables.

- relationship defines the relationship in the model and allows easy querying of related data.

You can now query posts belonging to a specific user, like so:

python

```python
user = db.query(User).filter(User.id == 1).first()
posts = user.posts
```

Conclusion

In this chapter, we explored how to connect databases to both **Django** and **FastAPI** in a full-stack development environment. We covered the differences between **SQL** and **NoSQL** databases, and when to use each. Then, we walked through using **Django ORM** to handle database operations, and **SQLAlchemy** with **FastAPI** for more flexible database interaction, including handling relationships between models and writing async database queries.

Now you have the foundational knowledge to integrate databases into your full-stack applications, making your back-end powerful and efficient while providing dynamic data to your React front-end. As you continue developing your application, understanding how to effectively query, manage, and secure your data will be essential to building robust web apps.

Chapter 8: Handling Real-Time Data with WebSockets and React

8.1 Understanding WebSockets

What Are WebSockets and Why Use Them?

WebSockets are a protocol that allows for **two-way communication** between a client (typically a web browser) and a server over a **single, persistent connection.** Unlike traditional HTTP, where the client sends a request and waits for a response, WebSockets enable continuous, real-time communication. This makes WebSockets ideal for applications that require fast, low-latency communication between the server and the client, such as real-time games, chat applications, and live notifications.

Key Characteristics of WebSockets:

1. **Full-Duplex Communication**: Both the client and the server can send and receive messages at any time.

2. **Persistent Connection**: Once a WebSocket connection is established, it remains open, allowing continuous data exchange without the need to repeatedly open new connections.

3. **Low Latency**: Since the connection is persistent, WebSockets provide much lower latency compared to polling or long-polling techniques.

When you open a WebSocket connection, it's like having a direct phone line between the client and the server, allowing both sides to speak to each other at any time without the delays that come from traditional HTTP requests.

Use Cases for Real-Time Communication (Chat, Notifications)

WebSockets are commonly used in applications where you need real-time data updates. Let's look at some common use cases:

1. **Chat Applications**: Chat apps, like Slack or WhatsApp, need to deliver messages instantly. WebSockets allow messages to be sent to the user as soon as they're received by the server, with no delay.

2. **Live Notifications**: Whether it's notifications about new emails, updates to a document, or social media alerts, WebSockets allow the server to notify users instantly when something happens.

3. **Live Data Feeds**: Applications like stock market tracking, sports apps, or news apps benefit from WebSockets to provide real-time updates without the need for refreshing the page.

4. **Collaborative Applications**: Applications that allow multiple users to collaborate in real-time, such as Google Docs or Trello, use WebSockets to update all users with changes as they happen.

Setting Up WebSocket Communication in Django and FastAPI

To use WebSockets with **Django** or **FastAPI**, you'll need a WebSocket library to handle communication.

WebSockets in Django

Django provides the Django Channels package for handling WebSockets and asynchronous communication.

1. **Install Django Channels**: First, install Django Channels:

```bash
pip install channels
```

2. **Set Up Channels in Django**: In settings.py, add 'channels' to the INSTALLED_APPS list and configure Channels as the default ASGI application:

```python
INSTALLED_APPS = [
    'django.contrib.admin',
    'django.contrib.auth',
    'django.contrib.contenttypes',
    'django.contrib.sessions',
```

```
    'django.contrib.messages',
    'django.contrib.staticfiles',
    'channels',  # Add channels
]
```

```
ASGI_APPLICATION =
'myproject.asgi.application'
```

3. **Create an ASGI Configuration**: Create an asgi.py file in your project directory:

```python
import os
from django.core.asgi import
get_asgi_application
from channels.routing import
ProtocolTypeRouter, URLRouter
from channels.auth import
AuthMiddlewareStack
```

```
os.environ.setdefault('DJANGO_SETT
INGS_MODULE',
'myproject.settings')


application = ProtocolTypeRouter({
    "http":
get_asgi_application(),
    "websocket":
AuthMiddlewareStack(
        URLRouter([
            # WebSocket routing
        ])
    ),
})
```

4. **Set Up a WebSocket Consumer:** A consumer is a Python class that handles WebSocket connections. Create a consumers.py file in your app:

```python
python
```

```python
from channels.generic.websocket
import AsyncWebsocketConsumer
import json


class
ChatConsumer(AsyncWebsocketConsume
r):
    async def connect(self):
        self.room_name =
"chat_room"
        self.room_group_name =
f"chat_{self.room_name}"

        # Join room group
        await
self.channel_layer.group_add(
            self.room_group_name,
            self.channel_name
        )
        await self.accept()
```

```python
    async def disconnect(self,
close_code):
        # Leave room group
        await
self.channel_layer.group_discard(
            self.room_group_name,
            self.channel_name
        )

    async def receive(self,
text_data):
        text_data_json =
json.loads(text_data)
        message =
text_data_json['message']

        # Send message to room
group
        await
self.channel_layer.group_send(
            self.room_group_name,
```

```python
            {
                'type':
'chat_message',
                'message': message
            }
        )


    async def chat_message(self,
event):
        message = event['message']

        # Send message to
WebSocket
        await
self.send(text_data=json.dumps({
            'message': message
        }))
```

5. **Routing WebSocket URLs**: In your routing.py, define the WebSocket route:

```python
python
```

```
from django.urls import path
from . import consumers


websocket_urlpatterns = [
    path('ws/chat/',
consumers.ChatConsumer.as_asgi()),
]
```

WebSockets in FastAPI

FastAPI supports WebSockets natively, using WebSocket from fastapi.

1. **Install FastAPI and Uvicorn**: First, install FastAPI and Uvicorn:

```bash
```

```bash
pip install fastapi uvicorn
```

2. **Set Up WebSocket in FastAPI**: Create a simple WebSocket endpoint in your FastAPI app:

```python
```

```
from fastapi import FastAPI,
WebSocket
from fastapi.responses import
HTMLResponse

app = FastAPI()

@app.get("/")
def get():
    html = """
    <html>
        <body>
            <h1>WebSocket
Test</h1>
            <form action=""
onsubmit="sendMessage(); return
false;">
                <input type="text"
id="messageText"
autocomplete="off"/>
```

```
<button>Send</button>
        </form>
        <ul id="messages">
        </ul>
        <script>
            var ws = new
WebSocket("ws://localhost:8000/ws"
);
            ws.onmessage =
function(event) {
                var messages =
document.getElementById("messages"
);
                var message =
document.createElement("li");

message.textContent = event.data;

messages.appendChild(message);
            };
```

```javascript
            function
sendMessage() {
                var input =
document.getElementById("messageTe
xt");

ws.send(input.value);
                input.value =
'';
            }
        </script>
    </body>
</html>
"""
    return HTMLResponse(html)


@app.websocket("/ws")
async def
websocket_endpoint(websocket:
WebSocket):
    await websocket.accept()
```

```
while True:
    data = await
websocket.receive_text()
    await
websocket.send_text(f"Message
received: {data}")
```

In the above example:

- The HTML page establishes a WebSocket connection to the FastAPI server.

- The JavaScript sends a message to the server, and the server responds with a message that gets displayed in the browser.

8.2 Implementing Real-Time Features in React

Integrating WebSockets with React Components

Now that we have WebSocket communication set up in Django and FastAPI, let's integrate WebSockets in a React front-end application.

1. **Setting Up WebSocket in React**: React doesn't have built-in support for WebSockets, but you can use the native WebSocket API in the browser to establish a WebSocket connection from the client.

Example of a simple React component using WebSocket:

```javascript
import React, { useEffect, useState } from 'react';
```

```
function Chat() {
  const [message, setMessage] =
useState('');
  const [messages, setMessages] =
useState([]);
  const ws = new
WebSocket('ws://localhost:8000/ws'
);

  useEffect(() => {
    ws.onmessage = (event) => {
      setMessages((prevMessages)
=> [...prevMessages, event.data]);
    };

    return () => {
      ws.close();
    };
  }, []);
```

```
  const handleSendMessage = () =>
{
    ws.send(message);
    setMessage('');
  };

  return (
    <div>
      <ul>
        {messages.map((msg, index)
=> (
          <li
key={index}>{msg}</li>
        ))}
      </ul>
      <input
        type="text"
        value={message}
        onChange={(e) =>
setMessage(e.target.value)}
```

```
    placeholder="Type a
message"
    />
    <button
onClick={handleSendMessage}>Send</
button>
  </div>
 );
}


export default Chat;
```

In this example:

- We create a WebSocket connection to ws://localhost:8000/ws (the URL where our FastAPI/Django WebSocket endpoint is hosted).

- We store incoming messages in the messages state and display them as a list.

- We send the user input to the server via the WebSocket connection when the "Send" button is clicked.

Handling Real-Time Data Updates in React

As you can see in the previous example, WebSockets allow us to handle real-time updates in React. Every time a new message is received, the onmessage event is triggered, and the setMessages function updates the state, causing the component to re-render and display the new message.

This allows the user interface to update instantly as new data arrives.

Managing State for Real-Time Features

Handling real-time data in React can sometimes lead to complex state management. You need to make sure that the component's state updates properly without unnecessary re-renders.

To avoid unnecessary re-renders, you can use React's **useRef** to store mutable values that don't trigger a re-render. For example, you can store the WebSocket connection in a ref to keep it persistent across renders without triggering component re-renders.

8.3 Building a Real-Time Chat Application

Setting Up WebSocket Communication in FastAPI/Django

We've already set up the WebSocket endpoints in both **Django** and **FastAPI**. Now, let's build a simple **real-time chat application** where users can send messages and see them instantly on the screen.

In Django:

We can build on the ChatConsumer we created earlier with Django Channels. Let's add functionality for multiple users to join the same chat room.

```python
class
ChatConsumer(AsyncWebsocketConsume
r):
    async def connect(self):
        self.room_name =
"chat_room"
        self.room_group_name =
f"chat_{self.room_name}"
```

```
        await
self.channel_layer.group_add(
            self.room_group_name,
            self.channel_name
        )
        await self.accept()

    async def disconnect(self,
close_code):
        await
self.channel_layer.group_discard(
            self.room_group_name,
            self.channel_name
        )

    async def receive(self,
text_data):
        text_data_json =
json.loads(text_data)
        message =
text_data_json['message']
```

```python
        await
self.channel_layer.group_send(
            self.room_group_name,
            {
                'type':
'chat_message',
                'message': message
            }
        )


    async def chat_message(self,
event):
        message = event['message']
        await
self.send(text_data=json.dumps({
            'message': message
        }))
```

In FastAPI:

FastAPI WebSocket implementation is already complete from the previous section. Let's use the same code to build a functional chat application.

Handling Messages and User Interactions

In both the FastAPI and Django implementations, the WebSocket connection allows for **bidirectional communication**, meaning users can send and receive messages without reloading the page. By sending messages from the client to the server, we can broadcast the messages to all connected clients, allowing real-time updates.

Styling the Chat App in React

For styling, you can use **CSS** or libraries like **styled-components** to give your chat app a polished look.

Example of simple CSS:

```css
css

.chat-container {
  display: flex;
  flex-direction: column;
  height: 300px;
  width: 400px;
  border: 1px solid #ccc;
  padding: 10px;
}

.messages {
  flex: 1;
  overflow-y: auto;
}

input[type="text"] {
  padding: 10px;
  width: 80%;
}
```

```
button {
  padding: 10px;
  width: 18%;
}
```

This creates a simple, clean layout for the chat app. The messages will scroll vertically, and the input field will allow the user to type and send messages.

Conclusion

In this chapter, we explored how to handle **real-time data** using **WebSockets** in both **Django** and **FastAPI**. We built a **real-time chat application** by integrating WebSocket communication between the back-end and the front-end (React).

We also discussed how to **manage state in React** for real-time features, handle real-time updates with WebSockets, and style the chat application to provide a user-friendly experience.

Real-time data and communication are essential features for modern web applications, and WebSockets offer a powerful and efficient way to achieve this. By mastering WebSockets, you can build highly interactive, live, and scalable applications such as messaging platforms, notifications, and collaborative tools.

Chapter 9: Testing Full-Stack Web Applications

9.1 The Importance of Testing in Web Development

Unit Tests vs Integration Tests vs End-to-End Tests

Testing is a fundamental part of web development, ensuring that your application works as expected, is bug-free, and provides a smooth user experience. There are several types of tests that play different roles in the testing process. These are mainly categorized into **unit tests, integration tests**, and **end-to-end (E2E) tests**. Understanding the distinctions between them is key to writing effective tests.

1. **Unit Tests**:

   ○ **Definition**: Unit tests are designed to test individual units of code, usually functions or methods. The goal is to isolate the smallest possible piece of functionality and verify that it behaves as expected.

   ○ **Why Use Unit Tests**: Unit tests help catch bugs early by ensuring that the individual parts of your application are functioning correctly. They are fast and can be run frequently.

Example:

python

```python
def add(a, b):
    return a + b

def test_add():
```

```
assert add(1, 2) == 3
assert add(-1, 1) == 0
```

2. **Integration Tests**:

- ○ **Definition**: Integration tests evaluate how different pieces of your application work together. They ensure that multiple components, such as database interactions, APIs, or services, interact correctly.

- ○ **Why Use Integration Tests**: They help verify that the system as a whole behaves as expected, especially when different components are connected.

Example:

```python
python
```

```python
def test_user_creation():
    response =
client.post("/users",
```

```
json={"name": "John", "email":
"john@example.com"})
    assert response.status_code ==
201
    assert response.json() ==
{"name": "John", "email":
"john@example.com"}
```

3. **End-to-End (E2E) Tests:**

   o **Definition**: End-to-end tests simulate real user interactions and test the entire application from the user's perspective. These tests are typically done through a browser or an automated tool like **Cypress** or **Selenium**.

   o **Why Use E2E Tests**: E2E tests ensure that all components, from the UI to the back-end, are integrated and functioning properly in a real-world environment.

Example:

```javascript
javascript

describe('User login', () => {
  it('should log in successfully with valid credentials', () => {
    cy.visit('/login');

    cy.get('input[name="username"]').type('john_doe');

    cy.get('input[name="password"]').type('password123');

    cy.get('button[type="submit"]').click();
    cy.url().should('include', '/dashboard');
```

```
});
});
```

By combining unit tests, integration tests, and E2E tests, you ensure that your application is thoroughly tested at different levels and that it meets both functional and performance expectations.

Testing Frameworks: Pytest, Jest, React Testing Library

Testing frameworks help you structure and automate your tests. They provide helpful features such as test runners, assertions, and mocking to make writing and executing tests easier.

1. **Pytest** (for Python/Django):

    o Pytest is a popular testing framework for Python that is simple to use, highly customizable, and has a rich ecosystem of plugins.

- ○ It supports fixtures, assertions, and running tests in parallel.

Example:

```python
import pytest

def test_addition():
    assert add(2, 3) == 5
```

2. **Jest** (for JavaScript/React):

- ○ Jest is a testing framework for JavaScript, commonly used with React applications. It provides an intuitive syntax, built-in mocking, and a powerful test runner.

Example:

```javascript
```

```javascript
test('should add two numbers', ()
=> {
  expect(add(2, 3)).toBe(5);
});
```

3. **React Testing Library**:

- React Testing Library is a tool that helps you test React components by simulating how users would interact with them. It encourages testing components from the user's perspective rather than testing implementation details.

Example:

```javascript
```

```javascript
import { render, screen } from
'@testing-library/react';
```

```
import App from './App';

test('renders learn react link',
() => {
  render(<App />);
  const linkElement =
screen.getByText(/learn react/i);

expect(linkElement).toBeInTheDocum
ent();
});
```

9.2 Writing Tests for the Back-End

Testing Django APIs with Pytest and Django Test Client

Django provides a test client that allows you to simulate requests to your views and test your

APIs. You can use **Pytest** to write more expressive and flexible tests.

1. **Setting Up Pytest**: First, install pytest-django:

bash

```
pip install pytest pytest-django
```

2. **Writing Tests for Django APIs**: Use the Django test client to simulate HTTP requests to your views.

Example:

python

```
import pytest
from django.urls import reverse
from rest_framework import status

@pytest.mark.django_db
def test_create_user():
```

```
url = reverse('user-list')
data = {"username": "john",
"email": "john@example.com"}
response = client.post(url,
data, format='json')
assert response.status_code ==
status.HTTP_201_CREATED
assert
response.data['username'] ==
"john"
```

In this example:

- We use reverse to get the URL for the user-list endpoint.

- We simulate a POST request to create a user and assert that the response status is 201 Created.

Writing Tests for FastAPI Routes

FastAPI also supports **Pytest** and allows you to use it for testing FastAPI routes. FastAPI provides an easy way to test routes with the TestClient.

1. **Setting Up Pytest for FastAPI**: Install pytest and httpx:

```bash
bash
```

```bash
pip install pytest httpx
```

2. **Writing Tests for FastAPI**: Example:

```python
python
```

```python
from fastapi.testclient import TestClient
from main import app  # Import your FastAPI app

client = TestClient(app)

def test_create_user():
    response =
client.post("/users/",
```

```
json={"username": "john", "email":
"john@example.com"})
    assert response.status_code ==
201
    assert
response.json()['username'] ==
"john"
```

FastAPI's TestClient simulates requests to the FastAPI app, making it easy to test APIs.

Testing Authentication and Security

Testing authentication and security is crucial to ensure that your app's security mechanisms work as expected.

- **Django**: You can use **pytest-django** to test authentication by simulating login and checking for protected routes.

Example of testing JWT authentication:

```python
```

```python
def
test_jwt_protected_route(client,
access_token):
    response =
client.get("/protected-route",
HTTP_AUTHORIZATION=f"Bearer
{access_token}")
    assert response.status_code ==
200
```

- **FastAPI**: Similarly, FastAPI's TestClient can be used to test protected routes by passing the **JWT** token in the headers.

Example:

```python
python
```

```python
def test_protected_route(client,
token):
    response =
client.get("/protected",
```

```
headers={"Authorization": f"Bearer
{token}"})
    assert response.status_code ==
200
```

9.3 Writing Tests for the Front-End

Unit Testing React Components with Jest

React components should be tested in isolation to ensure that each component behaves as expected. **Jest** is commonly used for unit testing React components.

1. **Setting Up Jest**: Install Jest and React Testing Library:

bash

```
npm install --save-dev jest
@testing-library/react
```

2. **Writing Tests for React Components**:
   Here's an example of a simple unit test for a React component:

```javascript

import { render, screen } from
'@testing-library/react';
import App from './App';


test('renders the heading', () =>
{
  render(<App />);
  const heading =
screen.getByRole('heading', {
name: /hello world/i });


expect(heading).toBeInTheDocument(
);
```

```
});
```

In this example:

- We render the App component.

- We use screen.getByRole to get the heading element and check if it's present in the document.

Simulating User Interactions in React Tests

React Testing Library allows you to simulate user interactions, such as clicks, form submissions, and typing.

Example of simulating a button click:

```javascript
import { render, screen, fireEvent } from '@testing-library/react';
import MyButton from './MyButton';
```

```
test('fires the onClick event', ()
=> {
  const handleClick = jest.fn();
  render(<MyButton
onClick={handleClick} />);
  const button =
screen.getByText('Click me');
  fireEvent.click(button);

expect(handleClick).toHaveBeenCall
edTimes(1);
});
```

Mocking API Calls in Tests

To avoid making real API calls during testing, you can **mock** the API responses. This helps to simulate how the app will behave with different data without actually hitting the back-end.

Example of mocking an API call:

```
javascript
```

```
import { render, screen, waitFor }
from '@testing-library/react';
import MyComponent from
'./MyComponent';

jest.mock('./api', () => ({
  fetchData:
jest.fn().mockResolvedValue({
data: 'mocked data' })
}));

test('displays data after API
call', async () => {
  render(<MyComponent />);
  await waitFor(() =>
screen.getByText(/mocked data/i));
  expect(screen.getByText(/mocked
data/i)).toBeInTheDocument();
});
```

In this example, we mock the fetchData function to return mocked data and test how the component reacts to that data.

9.4 Continuous Integration and Continuous Deployment (CI/CD)

Setting Up CI/CD Pipelines

Continuous Integration (CI) and **Continuous Deployment (CD)** are practices that help automate the process of testing, building, and deploying applications. CI/CD ensures that your code is always tested and deployed automatically when changes are made.

1. **Setting Up CI/CD with GitHub Actions**: GitHub Actions provides a powerful way to automate your workflow. You can use

GitHub Actions to set up CI/CD pipelines to run tests, build the project, and deploy it.

Here's an example of a simple GitHub Actions workflow to run tests:

```yaml
name: CI

on: [push]

jobs:
  test:
    runs-on: ubuntu-latest

    steps:
      - name: Checkout code
        uses: actions/checkout@v2

      - name: Set up Node.js
```

```
      uses: actions/setup-
node@v2
      with:
       node-version: '14'


   - name: Install dependencies
     run: npm install


   - name: Run tests
     run: npm test
```

In this workflow:

- o It checks out the code.

- o Sets up Node.js.

- o Installs dependencies and runs the tests.

2. **Automating Deployments**: You can also automate deployments to platforms like **Heroku, AWS**, or **DigitalOcean** by adding deployment steps to the pipeline.

Example of a GitHub Actions deployment step:

yaml

```
- name: Deploy to Heroku
  uses: akshnz/heroku-deploy-
action@v1
  with:
    heroku_api_key: ${{
secrets.HEROKU_API_KEY }}
    app_name: "my-app"
    branch: "main"
```

Automating Tests and Deployments

CI/CD ensures that your application is tested every time a change is pushed. This allows you to catch bugs early, as they are tested in an automated and consistent manner.

Conclusion

In this chapter, we've covered the importance of testing full-stack web applications. We learned about **unit tests**, **integration tests**, and **end-to-end tests** and how each one plays a vital role in ensuring the quality of your application. We then explored the various testing frameworks, such as **Pytest, Jest,** and **React Testing Library**, that make it easier to write and run tests for both back-end and front-end code.

We also covered how to set up and automate the process of **Continuous Integration and Continuous Deployment (CI/CD)**, helping to streamline testing, building, and deploying your applications.

Testing is a vital part of building reliable, scalable, and maintainable web applications. By implementing proper testing practices and

CI/CD pipelines, you ensure that your full-stack application remains robust as it grows.

Chapter 10: Optimizing Performance and Scaling Full-Stack Apps

10.1 Performance Optimization in Django and FastAPI

Performance is a key consideration in full-stack web applications. Whether you're building a small app or a large-scale enterprise system, optimizing your back-end APIs and database interactions is essential for ensuring that your application runs efficiently and can handle high traffic.

Database Query Optimization

Database queries can often become a bottleneck in web applications, especially as your database grows. Optimizing these queries is crucial for improving the overall performance of your app.

Django: Django's ORM makes it easy to work with databases, but it also has some built-in mechanisms that can lead to inefficient queries if not used properly. Here's how to optimize your database queries in Django:

1. **Use select_related and prefetch_related**: Django ORM executes additional queries when fetching related data. To reduce the number of queries, you can select_related (for foreign key and one-to-one relationships) and prefetch_related (for many-to-many relationships).

Example:

python

```python
# Without optimization
posts = Post.objects.all()
for post in posts:
    print(post.author.name)

# Optimized with select_related
posts = Post.objects.select_related('author').all()
for post in posts:
```

```
print(post.author.name)
```

2. **Avoid N+1 Query Problem**: The N+1 query problem occurs when you execute one query to retrieve records, but then perform an additional query for each record. This can quickly lead to a performance hit. Use select_related and prefetch_related to minimize the number of queries.

FastAPI: In FastAPI, you typically interact with the database using **SQLAlchemy**, which gives you full control over your queries.

1. **Avoid Unnecessary Queries**: Fetch only the data you need. For example, use **LIMIT** and **OFFSET** in **SQL** to paginate large datasets, reducing the memory load and response time.

2. **Use Asynchronous Queries**: FastAPI supports asynchronous programming,

which can be particularly useful when dealing with I/O-bound operations like database queries. Use async database queries to prevent the server from being blocked by database operations.

Example:

python

```python
from sqlalchemy.ext.asyncio import AsyncSession
from sqlalchemy.future import select

async def get_items(db: AsyncSession):
    result = await db.execute(select(Item).limit(10))
    return result.scalars().all()
```

Using Caching for Faster Responses

Caching is one of the most effective ways to speed up your application, especially for data that doesn't change often. By caching frequently requested data, you can reduce the number of calls to your database or API.

Django: Django provides several caching mechanisms such as **in-memory caching, file-based caching**, and **database caching**.

1. **In-Memory Caching**: The simplest form of caching is in-memory caching, which stores data in memory to avoid recalculating it on every request.

Example:

```python

from django.core.cache import cache
```

```
def get_user_profile(user_id):
    profile =
cache.get(f'user_profile_{user_id}
')
    if not profile:
        profile =
fetch_profile_from_database(user_i
d)

cache.set(f'user_profile_{user_id}
', profile, timeout=60*15)
    return profile
```

FastAPI: In FastAPI, caching can be done using third-party libraries such as **Redis**. Redis is a powerful, in-memory data structure store that can be used to cache frequently accessed data.

1. **Using Redis with FastAPI**: First, install the Redis package:

```bash
bash
```

```
pip install redis
Example:
python

import redis
from fastapi import FastAPI

app = FastAPI()
cache =
redis.Redis(host='localhost',
port=6379, db=0)

@app.get("/items/{item_id}")
async def get_item(item_id: int):
    item =
cache.get(f"item_{item_id}")
    if not item:
        item =
fetch_item_from_db(item_id)
```

```
cache.set(f"item_{item_id}", item,
ex=60*15)
    return item
```

Compressing API Responses and Static Files

Compression can significantly reduce the size of data sent over the network, leading to faster load times and reduced bandwidth usage.

Django: Django has built-in support for **gzip compression** of responses. You can enable this in your settings.py:

```python
MIDDLEWARE = [

'django.middleware.gzip.GZipMiddle
ware',  # Enable gzip compression
    ...
```

]

FastAPI: In FastAPI, you can use Gzip middleware for compressing API responses.

python

```
from fastapi import FastAPI
from fastapi.middleware.gzip
import GZipMiddleware

app = FastAPI()
app.add_middleware(GZipMiddleware,
minimum_size=1000)
```

This will automatically compress responses larger than 1000 bytes.

10.2   React   Performance Optimization

React is a powerful library for building user interfaces, but it can suffer from performance bottlenecks if not optimized properly. Here are some common techniques to optimize React performance.

Avoiding Unnecessary Re-Renders with React.memo

React components re-render every time their state or props change. However, unnecessary re-renders can harm performance, especially in large applications.

React.memo is a higher-order component that prevents unnecessary re-renders for components that receive the same props.

Example:

```javascript
const MyComponent =
React.memo(function
MyComponent(props) {
```

```
  console.log("Rendering:",
props.name);
  return <div>{props.name}</div>;
});
```

In this example, MyComponent will only re-render if its props.name changes. If the props remain the same, React will reuse the previous render and avoid unnecessary computation.

Lazy Loading Components

Lazy loading is a technique where components are loaded only when they are needed, which can reduce the initial load time of your application.

React's **React.lazy** allows you to dynamically import components only when they are required.

Example:

```javascript

import React, { Suspense } from
'react';
```

```
const MyComponent = React.lazy(()
=> import('./MyComponent'));

function App() {
  return (
    <Suspense
fallback={<div>Loading...</div>}>
      <MyComponent />
    </Suspense>
  );
}
```

In this example:

- React.lazy loads MyComponent only when it's needed.

- The Suspense component is used to show a fallback UI (e.g., a loading spinner) until the component is loaded.

Code Splitting with Webpack

Code splitting divides your code into smaller chunks, allowing only the necessary code to be loaded initially. This is typically done with **Webpack** in React.

React supports code splitting out of the box with React.lazy and Suspense, but Webpack also allows you to split your code manually for more control.

Example:

javascript

```javascript
import(/* webpackChunkName: "my-chunk-name" */ './MyComponent')
  .then(MyComponent => {
    // Use MyComponent here
  });
```

This will split the code for MyComponent into a separate file named my-chunk-name.js, and Webpack will load it only when needed.

10.3 Scaling Full-Stack Applications

As your application grows, it will need to handle increased traffic and larger amounts of data. Scaling is critical for maintaining performance under heavy load. Here's how you can scale your full-stack application.

Load Balancing and Horizontal Scaling

Load balancing is a technique used to distribute traffic across multiple servers. This ensures that no single server becomes overwhelmed and helps achieve **horizontal scaling**, which involves adding more servers to handle increasing traffic.

1. **Load Balancer**: A load balancer (such as **NGINX, HAProxy**, or **AWS Elastic Load Balancer**) is used to distribute incoming requests across multiple instances of your application.

2. **Horizontal Scaling**: You can horizontally scale your application by adding more application servers or database instances.

Handling Traffic Spikes with Auto-Scaling

Auto-scaling is a cloud-based technique where your application can automatically add or remove resources based on traffic demands. Services like **AWS Auto Scaling, Google Cloud AutoScaler**, and **Azure App Service** provide auto-scaling capabilities.

For example, you could set up an auto-scaling group that increases the number of server instances when CPU usage exceeds a certain threshold.

Using Docker for Containerization

Docker allows you to package your application into containers, which are lightweight, portable, and can run anywhere. Containers make it easier to scale applications and deploy them across multiple environments without worrying about differences between development, staging, and production systems.

Here's a simple example of how to Dockerize your app:

1. **Create a Dockerfile**:

```dockerfile
# Use the official Python image
from Docker Hub
FROM python:3.9-slim
```

```
# Set the working directory in the
container
WORKDIR /app

#  the dependencies file to the
container
 requirements.txt .

# Install dependencies
RUN pip install -r
requirements.txt

#  the rest of the application
code
 . .

# Run the application
CMD ["python", "app.py"]
```

2. **Build the Docker Image**:

```bash
bash
```

```
docker build -t myapp .
```

3. **Run the Docker Container**:

```
bash
```

```
docker run -p 5000:5000 myapp
```

Using Docker, you can deploy your app on different machines, or use orchestration tools like **Kubernetes** to manage the scaling of your containers.

Conclusion

In this chapter, we explored various techniques for optimizing and scaling your full-stack application. From database optimizations in Django and FastAPI to React performance improvements, these strategies ensure that your app performs well and can handle increased traffic.

We also covered scaling strategies like load balancing, auto-scaling, and containerization with Docker, which are essential for managing large-scale applications and ensuring high availability. By applying these techniques, you can create applications that not only perform well but also scale seamlessly to meet growing user demands.

Chapter 11: Securing Full-Stack Web Applications

11.1 Securing Your Backend API

When it comes to full-stack web applications, ensuring the security of your backend API is essential. Without proper protection, your backend can become a target for various types of attacks, including data breaches, unauthorized access, and malicious activity. Let's explore the key security measures you should take to secure your backend.

Implementing HTTPS and SSL/TLS

One of the most important steps in securing your backend is using **HTTPS (Hypertext Transfer**

Protocol Secure) instead of HTTP. HTTPS ensures that the data sent between the client and the server is encrypted, which protects sensitive information from being intercepted during transmission. This is achieved through **SSL/TLS (Secure Sockets Layer / Transport Layer Security)** certificates.

1. **Why HTTPS?**

    ○ **Encryption:** HTTPS encrypts data, making it difficult for third parties to read sensitive data like passwords, personal information, and credit card details.

    ○ **Integrity:** HTTPS ensures that data is not tampered with during transmission.

    ○ **Authentication:** HTTPS confirms that the server you're communicating with is the intended one, reducing the risk of man-in-the-middle attacks.

2. **How to Set Up SSL/TLS**:

   o **Obtain an SSL certificate** from a trusted certificate authority (CA) such as Let's Encrypt, which offers free SSL certificates.

   o **Install the certificate** on your server. For example, in a typical Apache or NGINX configuration, you'd add the certificate paths to your server configuration:

bash

```
ssl_certificate
/etc/ssl/certs/mydomain.crt;
ssl_certificate_key
/etc/ssl/private/mydomain.key;
```

- Once the certificate is installed, you can ensure that HTTPS is enforced by redirecting all HTTP traffic to HTTPS:

  - **NGINX**:

```bash
server {
    listen 80;
    server_name mydomain.com;
    return 301
https://$host$request_uri;
}
```

    - **Django**: In settings.py, enable the SECURE_SSL_REDIRECT option to force the app to redirect all HTTP traffic to HTTPS:

```python
```

```python
SECURE_SSL_REDIRECT = True
```

Using OAuth2 and JWT for Authentication

When it comes to securing access to your backend API, **OAuth2** and **JWT (JSON Web Tokens)** are two of the most common and widely accepted methods for handling authentication and authorization.

1. **OAuth2**: OAuth2 is an authorization framework that allows third-party services to exchange user credentials securely. OAuth2 involves two key parts:

   o **Access Tokens**: Short-lived tokens that grant access to a user's data.

- **Refresh Tokens**: Long-lived tokens used to obtain new access tokens once they expire.

To implement OAuth2 in Django or FastAPI, you can use third-party libraries like **Django OAuth Toolkit** or **FastAPI OAuth2**.

2. **JWT Authentication**: JWT is a compact, URL-safe token format that allows you to transmit claims (user data) between the client and server. JWT tokens are often used for **stateless authentication** in modern web apps, where the server does not need to store session information.

    - **Django JWT Authentication**: You can use the djangorestframework-simplejwt package for JWT authentication in Django.

bash

```
pip install djangorestframework-
simplejwt
```

Add the following to settings.py:

```python

REST_FRAMEWORK = {

'DEFAULT_AUTHENTICATION_CLASSES':
[

'rest_framework_simplejwt.authenti
cation.JWTAuthentication',
    ],
}
```

- o **FastAPI JWT Authentication**: FastAPI supports JWT authentication natively with the OAuth2PasswordBearer and JWT libraries. Example for FastAPI:

```python

from fastapi import FastAPI,
Depends
from fastapi.security import
OAuth2PasswordBearer
from jose import JWTError, jwt

app = FastAPI()

oauth2_scheme =
OAuth2PasswordBearer(tokenUrl="tok
en")

def get_current_user(token: str =
Depends(oauth2_scheme)):
    try:
        payload =
jwt.decode(token, "SECRET_KEY",
algorithms=["HS256"])
        return payload
```

```
except JWTError:
    raise
HTTPException(status_code=403,
detail="Could not validate
credentials")
```

Protecting Against SQL Injection and XSS Attacks

Two of the most common attacks on web applications are **SQL Injection** and **Cross-Site Scripting (XSS)**.

1. **SQL Injection**: SQL Injection occurs when an attacker inserts malicious SQL code into a query. This can lead to unauthorized access to your database, data leaks, or even deletion of records.

How to Protect Against SQL Injection:

- o **Use ORM libraries**: Django's ORM and SQLAlchemy in FastAPI automatically prevent SQL injection by using parameterized queries.

- o **Validate and Sanitize Input**: Always validate user input, particularly if you're dealing with raw SQL queries.

Example in Django:

python

```
# Safe query using Django ORM
user =
User.objects.get(id=user_id)
```

2. **XSS (Cross-Site Scripting)**: XSS attacks occur when an attacker injects malicious scripts into web pages that are then executed in the browser of other users.

How to Protect Against XSS:

- o **Escape User Inputs**: Make sure user-provided data is escaped before being rendered in HTML. Django's templating system automatically escapes variables, which helps prevent XSS.

- ○ **Content Security Policy (CSP)**: Implement a strong CSP to restrict the types of content that can be loaded in the browser.

11.2 Securing Your React Front-End

The security of your React front-end is just as important as the security of your backend. Here's how you can protect your React application from common security threats.

Preventing Cross-Site Scripting (XSS)

XSS attacks occur when an attacker injects malicious JavaScript into your application, which is then executed by other users. This is often achieved through form inputs, URLs, or any area where user input is reflected.

1. **Sanitize User Input**: Avoid rendering raw user input without sanitizing it first. Use libraries like **DOMPurify** or **sanitize-html** to ensure that HTML tags or JavaScript are not injected into the DOM.

2. **Escape Data Before Rendering**: React automatically escapes data in JSX, so you

don't need to worry about XSS when using React's rendering syntax. For example:

```jsx

```

```jsx
<div>{userInput}</div>
```

This prevents scripts from being executed, as React escapes the input to make it safe.

Protecting Against Cross-Site Request Forgery (CSRF)

CSRF is an attack where a malicious site makes a request to your web application on behalf of an authenticated user without their consent.

1. **Use Anti-CSRF Tokens**: CSRF tokens are used to verify that the request is coming from a legitimate source. Both Django and FastAPI support CSRF protection.

- **Django CSRF Protection**: By default, Django includes middleware for CSRF protection.

- **FastAPI CSRF Protection**: You can use third-party packages like fastapi_csrf_protect to handle CSRF tokens in FastAPI.

2. **SameSite Cookies**: Configure cookies to be SameSite to prevent them from being sent on cross-origin requests:

python

```
SESSION_COOKIE_SAMESITE = 'Strict'
# For Django
```

Secure Handling of Sensitive Data in React

It's important to handle sensitive data like passwords and tokens securely in your front-end application.

1. **Never Store Sensitive Data in Local Storage**: Avoid storing sensitive data such as JWT tokens in **localStorage** or **sessionStorage**, as they are vulnerable to XSS attacks. Instead, use **httpOnly cookies** to store tokens.

2. **Encrypt Sensitive Data**: For added security, encrypt sensitive data using libraries like **crypto-js**.

11.3 Best Practices for Secure Full-Stack Development

Security should be a top priority at every stage of full-stack web development. Here are some best practices to keep in mind:

Role-Based Access Control (RBAC)

RBAC is a method of restricting access to resources based on the roles assigned to users. This ensures that users can only access the parts of the application that they are authorized to.

1. **Define User Roles**: Create roles like admin, user, and guest, and assign appropriate permissions to each role.

2. **Enforce Role-Based Permissions**: Use role-based checks in both the backend and frontend to restrict access to certain actions or pages.

Example in Django:

python

```python
# Views with permission check
from django.contrib.auth.decorators import login_required, user_passes_test

@user_passes_test(lambda u: u.is_superuser)
def admin_view(request):
    return render(request, 'admin_dashboard.html')
```

Example in FastAPI:

python

```python
from fastapi import Depends, HTTPException
```

```
from fastapi.security import
OAuth2PasswordBearer


def get_current_user(token: str =
Depends(oauth2_scheme)):
    # Check the user role in the
database
    pass
```

Logging and Monitoring for Security Breaches

To ensure your application is secure, it's important to keep track of activities and monitor for potential breaches.

1. **Log All Security-Related Events**: Use logging frameworks to log events like failed login attempts, token generation, or changes to sensitive data. This can help in detecting suspicious activity.

2. **Set Up Real-Time Monitoring**: Use tools like **Prometheus**, **Grafana**, or **Datadog** to monitor the health of your application and alert you to potential breaches.

Regular Security Audits and Updates

Web application security is not a one-time task; it requires continuous attention. Regular security audits and updates ensure that your application remains secure over time.

1. **Update Dependencies**: Always use the latest, stable versions of libraries and frameworks, and ensure that any known vulnerabilities are patched.

2. **Automate Security Audits**: Use tools like **OWASP ZAP** or **Snyk** to perform automated security scans on your application.

3. **Penetration Testing**: Regularly conduct penetration testing to find and address vulnerabilities before malicious actors can exploit them.

Conclusion

In this chapter, we covered the essential strategies for securing full-stack web applications, from backend API security to React front-end security. By implementing HTTPS, OAuth2, JWT authentication, and protecting against attacks like SQL injection and XSS, you can significantly improve the security of your web applications.

Furthermore, we discussed best practices like role-based access control, logging, monitoring, and regular security audits to ensure that your app remains secure over time.

By following these practices, you can build applications that are not only functional but also resilient to security threats.

Chapter 12: Deploying Full-Stack Web Applications

12.1 Choosing the Right Deployment Platform

Comparing Deployment Services: Heroku, AWS, DigitalOcean

Deploying a full-stack web application involves choosing the right platform to host your project.

There are several popular deployment platforms, each with its own strengths and weaknesses. Let's compare **Heroku**, **AWS**, and **DigitalOcean** to help you make an informed decision based on your project's needs.

1. **Heroku**:

   o **Pros**:

      ▪ **Ease of Use**: Heroku is known for its simplicity and developer-friendly interface. It abstracts away much of the complexity of deployment, making it a great choice for beginners and rapid development cycles.

      ▪ **Integrated with Git**: Deploying to Heroku is as simple as pushing your code to a Git repository.

- **Pre-configured Add-ons**: It offers pre-configured add-ons for things like databases, caching, and monitoring.

○ **Cons**:

- **Scaling**: While Heroku is easy to use, it can become more expensive as your application scales. You might run into limits with storage, request handling, and server resources as your app grows.

- **Limited Customization**: For highly customized server configurations, you may find Heroku restrictive.

2. **AWS (Amazon Web Services):**

- **Pros:**

  - **Scalability**: AWS provides a wide range of services that allow you to scale your application as needed. It offers everything from basic computing resources to advanced machine learning and serverless architectures.

  - **Control**: With AWS, you get full control over your infrastructure. This is great if you need to fine-tune your environment for performance or cost-efficiency.

  - **Global Reach**: AWS offers data centers around the world, so you can deploy your application in regions close to your users for better performance.

- Cons:

  - **Complexity**: AWS comes with a steep learning curve. Setting up services like EC2 (Elastic Compute Cloud), RDS (Relational Database Service), or S3 (Simple Storage Service) requires more knowledge and configuration compared to platforms like Heroku.

  - **Cost**: AWS can become quite expensive if not properly managed, especially if your application scales significantly.

3. **DigitalOcean:**

- **Pros:**

  - **Simplicity with Power:** DigitalOcean is easier to use than AWS but more powerful than Heroku. It provides virtual private servers (called Droplets) that allow for a more customized deployment environment.

  - **Cost-Effective:** DigitalOcean is generally cheaper than AWS and offers a clear pricing structure, which is ideal for smaller to medium-sized applications.

  - **Managed Databases:** DigitalOcean also offers

managed databases, making it easier to set up and scale databases without managing them yourself.

- ○ **Cons:**

  - ▪ **Manual Setup:** While DigitalOcean is more straightforward than AWS, it still requires you to manage things like virtual servers, storage, and load balancing. You'll need to do more configuration than with Heroku.

Understanding Docker for Containerization

When deploying full-stack applications, it's important to ensure that your app runs consistently across different environments. **Docker** provides a solution to this problem by containerizing your application.

What is Docker?

- Docker is a platform that allows you to package your application along with all its dependencies into a **container**. A container is a lightweight, portable, and self-sufficient unit that can run anywhere—on your local machine, a cloud server, or even on a different operating system.

Why Use Docker?

- **Consistency Across Environments**: Docker containers ensure that the application will run the same way in development, testing, staging, and production.

- **Isolation**: Each component (e.g., front-end, back-end, database) can run in its own container, ensuring no conflicts between dependencies.

- **Scalability**: Docker containers are easy to scale. You can deploy multiple instances of the same container as needed.

Setting Up Docker:

1. Install Docker on your system (follow the official guide for your operating system).

2. Create a Dockerfile for your project. Here's an example for a **React** app:

```
dockerfile

FROM node:14

WORKDIR /app
 . /app

RUN npm install
RUN npm run build

EXPOSE 3000
```

```
CMD ["npm", "start"]
```

3. Build and run the Docker container:

```
bash
```

```
docker build -t my-react-app .
docker run -p 3000:3000 my-react-app
```

With Docker, you can easily deploy your full-stack application to any platform that supports Docker, including **AWS**, **Heroku**, and **DigitalOcean**.

Setting Up Continuous Deployment with GitHub Actions

Continuous Deployment (**CD**) allows you to automatically deploy your application whenever new code is pushed to your repository. **GitHub Actions** provides an easy way to set up CI/CD pipelines directly from your GitHub repository.

Setting Up GitHub Actions:

1. Create a .github/workflows/deploy.yml file in your repository.

2. Define the steps for deployment, such as installing dependencies, building the app, running tests, and deploying.

Example GitHub Actions workflow:

```yaml
name: Deploy to Heroku

on:
  push:
    branches:
      - main

jobs:
  deploy:
    runs-on: ubuntu-latest
```

```
steps:
  - name: Checkout Code
    uses: actions/checkout@v2

  - name: Set up Node.js
    uses: actions/setup-node@v2
    with:
      node-version: '14'

  - name: Install Dependencies
    run: npm install

  - name: Build React App
    run: npm run build

  - name: Deploy to Heroku
    uses: akshnz/heroku-deploy-action@v1
    with:
```

```
        heroku_api_key: ${{
secrets.HEROKU_API_KEY }}
        app_name: 'my-react-app'
        branch: 'main'
```

In this example:

- The workflow is triggered every time code is pushed to the main branch.

- It installs dependencies, builds the React app, and deploys it to **Heroku** using a pre-built GitHub action.

12.2 Preparing Your Application for Production

Configuring Django and FastAPI for Production

Before deploying your Django or FastAPI application to production, you must configure certain settings to optimize performance, security, and stability.

Django Production Configuration

1. **Security Settings**:

   - Set DEBUG = False in settings.py.

   - Set ALLOWED_HOSTS to include the production domain:

```python

ALLOWED_HOSTS = ['mywebsite.com', 'www.mywebsite.com']
```

2. **Database Configuration**:

   - Use a production database (e.g., PostgreSQL) instead of SQLite. Update DATABASES in settings.py with production credentials.

3. **Static and Media Files**:

- ○ Use **WhiteNoise** or a similar package to serve static files in production. Configure the static and media directories:

```python
STATIC_URL = '/static/'
STATIC_ROOT =
os.path.join(BASE_DIR,
'staticfiles')


MEDIA_URL = '/media/'
MEDIA_ROOT =
os.path.join(BASE_DIR, 'media')
```

4. **Using Gunicorn as the Application Server**:

- ○ Use **Gunicorn** (Green Unicorn) as the production server:

```bash
```

```
pip install gunicorn
gunicorn
myproject.wsgi:application
```

FastAPI Production Configuration

1. **Security Settings**:

   o FastAPI doesn't require extensive configuration for security, but ensure you're using HTTPS and have proper **CORS** settings if your app communicates with a front-end.

2. **Database Configuration**:

   o Configure your production database (PostgreSQL, MySQL, etc.) in the settings and use **SQLAlchemy** for database operations.

3. **Using Uvicorn for Production**:

o In production, use **Uvicorn** with **Gunicorn** to serve FastAPI applications.

```bash
pip install gunicorn uvicorn
gunicorn -w 4 -k
uvicorn.workers.UvicornWorker
myapp:app
```

Minifying React Code for Faster Load Times

To optimize your front-end application for production, you need to **minify** and **bundle** your React code. This reduces file sizes, improving load times and overall performance.

1. **Minifying with Webpack**: React's build process, using **Webpack**, automatically

minifies your code for production. You can run:

```bash
npm run build
```

2. **Lazy Loading**: Implement lazy loading to only load the parts of your app when needed, further improving performance.

Example:

```javascript
const MyComponent = React.lazy(()
=> import('./MyComponent'));
```

Environment Variables and Secrets Management

Managing sensitive information, such as API keys, database credentials, and other secrets, is crucial. Environment variables provide a secure way to store this information.

1. **Environment Variables in Django**: Use libraries like **django-environ** to manage environment variables. Set the environment variables in a .env file:

bash

```
SECRET_KEY=mysecretkey
DATABASE_URL=postgres://user:password@localhost/dbname
```

2. **Environment Variables in FastAPI**: Use **Pydantic** to handle environment variables in FastAPI. You can load variables using python-dotenv:

bash

```
pip install python-dotenv
```

Then in your code:

```python

from pydantic import BaseSettings

class Settings(BaseSettings):
    db_url: str
    secret_key: str
```

These variables should be set in your deployment environment, and they can be accessed securely in production.

12.3 Deploying and Maintaining Your Web App

Setting Up Databases in the Cloud

Cloud databases allow you to scale your application while ensuring that data is highly available and secure.

1. **PostgreSQL on Heroku:**

- You can easily add a PostgreSQL database to your Heroku application with:

```bash
heroku addons:create heroku-postgresql:hobby-dev
```

- This will automatically set the DATABASE_URL environment variable in Heroku, which you can use in your Django or FastAPI app.

2. **PostgreSQL on AWS**:

- AWS provides **RDS (Relational Database Service)** to manage databases. You can create a PostgreSQL instance through the AWS console and connect it to your application.

3. **DigitalOcean Managed Databases**:

○ DigitalOcean offers managed databases for PostgreSQL, MySQL, and Redis. You can provision a managed database and connect it to your application with minimal configuration.

Monitoring and Maintaining Your Deployed App

Once your application is live, it's important to monitor it for performance issues, errors, and downtime.

1. **Logging**:

   ○ Use logging libraries like **Sentry**, **LogRocket**, or **New Relic** to track errors and performance in your application.

2. **Uptime Monitoring**:

o Use tools like **UptimeRobot** or **Pingdom** to monitor your app's uptime and ensure that it's available for users.

Handling Downtime and Error Logs

In the event of an issue, it's crucial to have a plan for handling downtime and analyzing error logs:

1. **Graceful Shutdown**:

   o Ensure that your application gracefully handles shutdowns, whether planned (e.g., during deployments) or unplanned (e.g., server crashes).

2. **Error Logs**:

   o Log any errors that occur in your application, and use a logging system that allows you to analyze and fix these errors quickly.

Conclusion

In this chapter, we covered the entire process of deploying a full-stack web application. We discussed how to choose the right deployment platform (Heroku, AWS, DigitalOcean) based on your project's needs. We also explored how to prepare your application for production, optimize performance, and manage environment variables.

We then looked at deploying and maintaining your app in the cloud, setting up databases, monitoring performance, and handling error logs. By following these best practices, you'll ensure that your full-stack web application is ready for production and can scale effectively.

With this knowledge, you now have the tools to deploy, monitor, and maintain a robust, production-ready full-stack web application.

Chapter 13: Conclusion: The Journey Ahead

13.1 The Road to Becoming a Full-Stack Developer

What You've Learned and Accomplished

Over the course of this journey, you have gained valuable skills that will help you build robust, scalable, and interactive web applications. From understanding front-end technologies like **React** to mastering back-end frameworks such as **Django** and **FastAPI**, you now have the knowledge to create full-stack applications that are both functional and well-architected.

Here's a recap of what you've learned:

1. **Front-End Development:**

   o **React:** You've learned how to build dynamic user interfaces using React components, manage state, and handle events.

   o **React Router:** You can now implement client-side routing to create single-page applications (SPAs).

   o **React Testing:** You've acquired the skills to write tests for React components using Jest and React Testing Library to ensure that your UI behaves as expected.

2. Back-End Development:

- **Django**: You've explored Django's model-view-template (MVT) architecture, setting up databases with the Django ORM, writing API endpoints, and securing your application.

- **FastAPI**: You've learned how to build high-performance, asynchronous APIs with FastAPI and connect it to databases using SQLAlchemy.

- **Authentication**: You now know how to handle user authentication, including the implementation of

JWT (JSON Web Tokens) for secure login processes.

3. **Database Management:**

- **Relational Databases:** You've worked with relational databases like PostgreSQL and MySQL, using Django's ORM and SQLAlchemy to manage data.

- **Real-Time Communication:** You've explored how to integrate real-time data with WebSockets and how to implement features like chat applications.

4. **Deployment:**

- **Deploying Applications:** You've learned how to deploy both front-end and back-end applications on cloud platforms like **Heroku, AWS,** and **DigitalOcean.**

- ○ **CI/CD**: You've understood the importance of continuous integration and continuous deployment, setting up pipelines using GitHub Actions to automate testing and deployment processes.

- ○ **Monitoring**: You've learned to monitor your deployed applications, track errors, and maintain uptime for production applications.

By completing this journey, you've equipped yourself with a well-rounded skill set, enabling you to confidently build full-stack web applications and understand the entire software development lifecycle—from building the app to deploying it in the cloud.

Next Steps for Continuing Your Journey

Although you have accomplished a great deal, the journey to becoming a proficient full-stack developer doesn't end here. In fact, this is just the beginning of your learning path. The field of web development is constantly evolving, and there's always more to learn. Here are some next steps to continue improving your skills:

1. **Deepen Your Knowledge:**

   o **Advanced React:** Explore **React hooks** in more depth, experiment with **Context API** for state management, and delve into **React Native** for mobile app development.

   o **Explore Back-End Frameworks:** If you're interested in more options for back-end development, consider learning **Node.js**, **Express.js**, or **Ruby on Rails**. This will give you a broader understanding of the tools available.

o **Master Databases**: Learn more about database management by diving into advanced topics like database optimization, indexing, and using **NoSQL** databases like **MongoDB** for non-relational data.

2. **Build More Projects**: The best way to reinforce what you've learned is through practice. Build more **real-world projects** that involve both front-end and back-end development. For example:

o A **task manager app** that allows users to create, update, and delete tasks.

- A **social media platform** where users can share posts, like and comment on them.

- A **e-commerce site** with user authentication, product listings, a shopping cart, and an order history page.

3. **Contribute to Open Source**: Open-source projects provide a fantastic opportunity to collaborate with other developers, contribute to real-world projects, and learn from others. Platforms like **GitHub** are filled with open-source projects where you can help fix bugs, improve documentation, or add features.

4. **Stay Updated:**

- Follow blogs, podcasts, and tutorials from reputable sources such as

Medium, **Dev.to**, **freeCodeCamp**, and **Traversy Media** to stay up-to-date with the latest trends and best practices in web development.

5. **Join Developer Communities**:

   ○ Engage with other developers by joining communities like **Stack Overflow**, **Reddit**, **Dev.to**, or **Twitter**. Participating in these communities will allow you to get feedback on your code, ask for help when you get stuck, and discover new resources.

By continuing to learn and build projects, you will become a well-rounded full-stack developer capable of tackling complex, real-world problems.

Additional Resources for Full-Stack Development

To further your learning, here are some excellent resources for full-stack development:

1. **Books**:

   - **"Eloquent JavaScript"** by Marijn Haverbeke – A great resource for learning JavaScript.

   - **"You Don't Know JS"** by Kyle Simpson – Deep dive into JavaScript for experienced developers.

   - **"Django for Beginners"** by William S. Vincent – A beginner-friendly book for mastering Django.

   - **"Learning React"** by Alex Banks and Eve Porcello – A comprehensive guide to React.

2. **Online Courses:**

   - **freeCodeCamp** – Offers comprehensive, free full-stack web development courses.

   - **Udemy** – Provides a wide range of paid and free courses on full-stack web development.

   - **Codecademy** – Offers interactive lessons in full-stack development.

3. **Documentation:**

   - **React Docs:** https://reactjs.org/docs/getting-started.html

   - **Django Docs:** https://docs.djangoproject.com/en/stable/

- o **FastAPI** **Docs:**
https://fastapi.tiangolo.com/

4. **Community Platforms:**

- o **Stack Overflow** – A go-to platform for getting answers to your coding questions.

- o **GitHub** – Host and collaborate on open-source projects.

- o **Dev.to** – A community of developers sharing insights, tutorials, and discussions.

13.2 Real-World Applications of Full-Stack Skills

Industries That Rely on Full-Stack Development

Full-stack developers are in high demand across various industries due to their ability to work on both front-end and back-end technologies. Some key industries that rely on full-stack development include:

1. **Tech and Software Development:**

   o Full-stack developers are highly sought after in tech companies for building applications from start to finish. Whether it's building a **content management system, social media platform,** or **collaborative tools,** tech companies need developers who can handle both the user interface and back-end logic.

2. **E-Commerce:**

   o The e-commerce industry relies on full-stack developers to build and maintain online stores, manage inventory, integrate payment gateways, and handle user authentication.

3. **Finance and FinTech:**

   o Full-stack developers are essential in the finance sector for developing secure platforms for online banking, payments, and financial data analysis.

4. **Healthcare:**

   o In healthcare, full-stack developers are needed to build secure systems for patient data management, online consultations, and electronic health records (EHR).

5. **Entertainment and Media**:

- ○ Full-stack developers work on platforms that host streaming services, news websites, and online gaming systems. These applications often require complex front-end and back-end integration.

6. **Startups and Freelance**:

- ○ Startups often prefer full-stack developers because they can manage both the front-end and back-end, which makes them highly valuable in early-stage projects with limited resources. Freelancers in the web development field also find full-stack skills essential for building end-to-end solutions for clients.

Building Projects for Portfolio and Freelance Work

As a full-stack developer, building a **strong portfolio** is one of the most effective ways to showcase your skills and attract potential clients or employers. Here are some project ideas to help you build a standout portfolio:

1. **To-Do List Application:**

   o A simple but effective way to demonstrate your skills. It can include user authentication, the ability to add and delete tasks, and store tasks in a database.

2. **Blog Platform:**

- Build a full-fledged blogging platform where users can create, edit, and delete posts. Add features like commenting and liking posts to showcase your ability to handle dynamic content.

3. **E-Commerce Website**:

- A simple e-commerce website with a product catalog, shopping cart, and checkout process. This can demonstrate your understanding of payments and secure transactions.

4. **Social Media App**:

- A basic social media platform where users can post updates, follow others, and like/share content. This showcases your skills in user authentication, database management, and front-end development.

5. **Job Board**:

  ○ A job listing website where users can post job openings, apply for positions, and filter jobs by category, location, etc. This can demonstrate your ability to manage complex data and create a user-friendly interface.

Make sure to **deploy** your projects and **document** them well, including a README file with project details, the technologies used, and the features implemented.

Opportunities for Contributing to Open Source Projects

Contributing to open-source projects is an excellent way to gain experience, build your reputation as a developer, and collaborate with others. It's also a great way to stay engaged with the developer community. Here are some steps for getting started with open source:

1. **Find Projects:**

   o Use platforms like **GitHub** or **GitLab** to find open-source projects in need of contributions. Look for projects that interest you or that align with the technologies you want to learn.

2. **Start Small:**

   o Start by tackling smaller issues or bugs. Many open-source projects label easy issues with tags like "beginner-friendly" or "good first issue."

3. **Make Contributions:**

- o Fork the project, make your changes, and create a pull request (**PR**). Communicate clearly with the maintainers and follow the contribution guidelines.

4. **Join Developer Communities**:

- o Platforms like **Dev.to**, **Reddit** (r/learnprogramming), and **Stack Overflow** can help you connect with others and find open-source opportunities.

Contributing to open source not only boosts your portfolio but also helps you learn best practices, improve your coding skills, and stay up-to-date with the latest technologies.

Conclusion

The journey to becoming a full-stack developer is a rewarding one, filled with learning, problem-solving, and constant improvement. You've acquired a comprehensive skill set—from building the front-end with React to managing databases with Django and FastAPI, deploying applications, and setting up CI/CD pipelines.

As you continue to grow in your career, building projects, contributing to open-source, and staying curious will help you succeed in the ever-evolving world of web development. Whether you're working for a company, freelancing, or starting your own venture, the possibilities are endless for a full-stack developer who is passionate about learning and building great products.

So, take the next steps with confidence, keep honing your skills, and remember: the journey of learning never truly ends!